Realizing
SOUL

Realizing SOUL

From Intuition to an Inspired Life

Selected and compiled
from the writings of

Paul Brunton

by Robert Larson

Larson Publications
Burdett, New York

ISBN-10: 1-936012-32-4
ISBN-13: 978-1-936012-32-9
Library of Congress Control Number: 2015939057

Publisher's Cataloging-In-Publication Data
(Prepared by The Donohue Group, Inc.)
Brunton, Paul, 1898-1981.
    [Notebooks of Paul Brunton. Selections. 2015]
    Realizing soul : from intuition to an inspired life / selected and compiled from the writings of Paul Brunton by Robert Larson.
     pages ; cm

    "Published for the Paul Brunton Philosophic Foundation."
    Contains selections from: The notebooks of Paul Brunton.
    Issued also as an ebook.
    ISBN-13: 978-1-936012-32-9
    ISBN-10: 1-936012-32-4

    1. Spiritual life. 2. Soul. 3. Awareness--Religious aspects. 4. Meditations. I. Larson, Robert, 1930- II. Paul Brunton Philosophic Foundation. III. Title. IV. Title: Notebooks of Paul Brunton. Selections. 2015

BL624 .B692 2015
204/.4   2015939057

Published for the Paul Brunton Philosophic Foundation
by Larson Publications
4936 NYS Route 414
Burdett, New York 14818 USA
larsonpublications.com

24 23 22 21 20 19 18 17 16 15
10 9 8 7 6 5 4 3 2 1

Contents

Introduction

Paul Brunton (1898–1981) is an enlightened philosopher and author from our own time. From his pen have come more than thirty books. They address a broad spectrum of key issues we meet in the process of becoming conscious of, deepening, and developing our spirituality. During the last thirty years of his life, he wrote daily but published nothing.

After Paul Brunton passed away, these later writings were carefully sorted and compiled by students of the philosopher/author Anthony Damiani at Wisdom's Goldenrod Center for Philosophic Studies, in Valois, New York. The results of their work appeared from 1982–1987 as a series of sixteen volumes entitled *The Notebooks of Paul Brunton,* which comprehensively treats all aspects of the spiritual quest.

Since 2010, a new text selection from *The Notebooks* has been offered daily in fifteen languages at *www.paulbruntondailynote.se* on the Internet. All selections that appear on this site can be read or listened to without cost. The Swedish Paul Brunton Philosophic Foundation administers this service. *Realizing Soul* presents a sampling of the first four years' publication of such selections on the Internet.

A few introductory words may be helpful about what this book contains.

Paradoxically, we live on two levels of consciousness without knowing our situation. The lower—the ego level—is familiar. The higher, which Paul Brunton speaks of as Overself and many other people speak of as soul, is unknown for most of us. The Overself is our real identity.

We do not realize this because we are captured in an illusion, the ego illusion. To be able to realize our real identity, we must first understand what we are not.

Intuition is the Overself's gentle language. All of us have intuitions, but only some of us are conscious of what is happening when these intuitions come. This is our great dilemma.

People who have been granted a glimpse of the Overself know by their own unforgettable experience that there is something beyond the ego, and that it is worth longing for more than anything else. These glimpses come and go, but they do confirm the reality and presence of the Overself. And they give a foretaste of permanent, unbroken awakening.

An intuition can be prolonged and deepened to a glimpse. A glimpse in turn can be prolonged and deepened into full spiritual awakening.

When we finally understand our situation, we see that this kind of awakening is the higher purpose of our lives. Then the question arises, How can it be realized. Many of us at this stage discover that there is a long and noble tradition known as the spiritual quest, and that it consists of two parts. In the first stage, called the Long Path, the quester becomes a new person. In the second, called the Short Path, that new person can be blessed at any moment with the grace of lasting enlightenment.

Our own efforts bring us closer to the awakening but cannot produce it. The divine grace leads us as far as we can go on our own, and then completes what we cannot complete on our own.

Consciously or unconsciously, we all long for this liberation.

The Notebooks of Paul Brunton contain more than 34,000 texts. *Realizing Soul* gives only a limited introduction to certain parts of Paul Brunton's magnificent work. For explanations of unfamiliar terms in his writing and/or more information about his work, please visit http://paulbrunton.org.

ROBERT LARSON
APRIL 2015

The day will inexorably come when this pen shall move no more and I wish therefore to leave on record, for the benefit of those who shall come after, a sacred and solemn testimony that I know—as surely as I know that I am not this pen which scribes these lines—that a being, benign, wise, protective, and divine, whom men call the Soul, whom I call the Overself, truly exists in the hearts of all; therefore all may discover it. . . . For the presence of man's own innermost divinity is the guarantee that he must inescapably seek and find it.

1

The Mystery

All these little minds which people the universe and are active in Nature's kingdoms could not have come into being unless there were a universal originating Mind. They point to its existence, silently speak of their divine Source. The materialistic notion that individual centres of intelligent life could have been produced by non-intelligent "matter" is an utter absurdity.

The human situation is a paradox. We are at one and the same time inhabitants of a world of reality as well as a world of appearance. A true human life must embrace both aspects, must be spiritual as well as physical, must integrate the intuitive as well as the intellectual.

He has a double existence, with the frontal part of his consciousness in time and the real part out of it. All the miseries and misfortunes which may enter into the one part will make no difference to the blessed tranquillity which permanently reigns in the other.

The Overself

. . . The Overself is a term of which past experience may furnish no meaning. But perhaps you have had strangely beautiful moments when everything seemed to be still, when an ethereal world of being seemed very near to you. Well, in those moments you were lifted up to the Overself. . . .

Overself is the inner or true self of man, reflecting the divine being and attributes. The Overself is an emanation from the ultimate reality but is neither a division nor a detached fragment of it. It is a ray shining forth but not the sun itself.

. . . If anyone could imagine a consciousness which does not objectify anything but remains in its own native purity, a happiness beyond which it is impossible to go, and a self which is unvaryingly one and the same, he would have the correct idea of the Overself. . . .

. . . Human beings are rooted in the ultimate mind through the Overself, which therefore partakes on the one hand of a relationship with a vibratory world and on the other of an existence which is above all relations. . . .

Neither the senses nor the intellect can tell us anything about the intrinsic nature of this Infinite Mind. Nevertheless we are not left in total ignorance about it. From its manifestation, the cosmos, we may catch a hint of its Intelligence. From its emanation, the soul, we may catch more than a hint of its Beneficence. "More than," I say, because the emanation may be felt within us as our very being whereas the manifestation is outside us and is apart.

Everything that exists in time must also exist in change. The Overself does not exist in time and is not subject to change.

This is the abiding essence of a man, his true self as against his ephemeral person. Whoever enters into its consciousness enters into timelessness, a wonderful experience where the flux of pleasures and pains comes to an end in utter serenity, where regrets for the past, impatience at the present, and fears of the future are unknown.

We all think, experience, feel, and identify with the "I." But who really knows what it is? To do this we need to look inside the mind, not at what it contains, as psychologists do, but at what it is in itself. If we persevere, we may find the "I" behind the "I."

He will feel that this nobler self actually overshadows him at times. This is literally true. Hence we have named it the Overself.

That element in his consciousness which enables him to understand that he exists, which causes him to pronounce the words, "I Am," is the spiritual element, here called Overself. It is really his basic self for the three activities of thinking feeling and willing are derived from it, are ripples spreading out of it, are attributes and functions which belong to it. But as we ordinarily think feel and act, these activities do not express the Overself because they are under the control of a different entity, the personal ego.

There is only one Overself for the whole race, but the point of contact with it is special and unique, and constitutes man's higher individuality.

There is some point in each individual being where the human and the divine must join, where man's little consciousness bends low before, or blends subtly with, the Universal Mind which is his ultimate source. It is impossible to describe that intersection in any terms which shall adequately fit it, but it can be named. In philosophy it is the Overself.

That which connects the individual man to the Universal Spirit, I call the Overself. This connection can never be broken. Its existence is the chief guarantee that there is hope of salvation for *all*, not merely for those who think their group alone will be granted it.

This is the paradox, that the Overself is at once universal and individual. It is the first because it overshadows all men as a single power. It is the second because it is found by each man within himself. It is both space and the point in space. It is infinite Spirit and yet it is also the holy presence in everyone's heart.

. . . Outwardly all differ but in the deepest root of consciousness all are the same.

The mysterious character of the Overself inevitably puzzles the intellect. We may appreciate it better if we accept the paradoxical fact that it unites a duality and that therefore there are two ways of thinking of it, both correct. There is the divine being which is entirely above all temporal concerns, absolute and universal, and there is also the demi-divine being which is in historical relation with the human ego.

No one can explain what the Overself is, for it is the origin, the mysterious source, of the explaining mind, and beyond all its capacities. But what can be explained are the effects of standing consciously in its presence, the conditions under which it manifests, the ways in which it appears in human life and experience, the paths which lead to its realization.

We cannot see, hear, or touch without the mind. But the mind, in its turn, cannot function or even exist without the Overself.

It is this grandeur of self that is the magnetic pole drawing us to the Good, the Beautiful, the Just, the True, and the Noble. Yet itself is above all these attributes for it is the Attributeless, the Ineffable, and the Infinite that human thought cannot grasp.

The Overself is neither a cold metaphysical concept nor a passing wave of emotion. It is a Presence—sublime, sacred, and beneficent—which grips your heart, thought, and body by its own mysterious power, making you regard life from a nobler standpoint.

The Overself is not merely a pleasant feeling—although it arouses such a feeling—but a veritable force. When it possesses a man, he is literally and actually gripped by a dynamic energy. A creative power henceforth pervades his atmosphere, enters his deeds, permeates his mind and charges his words, and runs through his history.

That the Overself is not the product of an inflated imagination but has a real existence, is a truth which any man who has the required patience and submits to the indispensable training may verify himself.

. . . We can know the Overself only by *being* it, not by thinking it. It is beyond thoughts for it is Thought, Pure Mind, itself.

. . . The day will come when science, waking more fully than it is now from its materialistic sleep, will confess humbly that the soul of man does really exist. . . .

To the man of insight there is something strange, ironic, and yet pathetic in the spectacle of those who turn the consciousness and the understanding derived from Overself against the acknowledgment of Its existence.

This is its mystery, that seeing all, it is itself seen by none.

The Kingdom of Heaven Is within

What we are ordinarily conscious of are the thoughts and feelings of the ego, but there is much more in us than that. There is the true self, of which the ego is only a miserable caricature. If we could penetrate to this, the fundamental element of our selfhood, we would never again be satisfied with a wholly egoistic life—

Hidden away in every man there exists a being immeasurably superior to the ordinary person that he is.

There is a hidden light within man himself. Sometimes its glow appears in his most beautiful art productions, his loftiest religious revelations, his most irreproachable moral decisions.

There is a strange feeling that not he but somebody else is living and talking in the same body. It is somebody nobler and wiser than his own ego.

He feels the Presence of something higher than himself, wise, noble, beautiful, and worthy of all reverence. Yet it is really himself—the best part come at last into unfoldment and expression.

If we lack the capacity to comprehend, gauge, or perceive the Infinite, we do have the capacity to feel its presence intuitively.

❦

. . . That which he has been seeking so ardently has been within himself all the time. For there at the core of his being, hidden away underneath all the weakness, passion, pettiness, fear, and ignorance, dwells light, love, peace, and truth. The windows of his heart open on eternity, only he has kept them closed! He is as near the sacred spirit of God as he ever shall be, but he must open his eyes to see it. Man's divine estate is there deep within himself. But he must claim it.

❦

Out of this deep mysterious centre within himself, he will draw the strength to endure distresses with fortitude, the wisdom to manage situations without after-regrets, the insight to keep the great and little values of everyday living in proper perspective.

❦

The feeling of some presence inside his heart will become so powerful at intervals, so real and so intense, that he will quite naturally enter into conversation with it. He will implore it, pray to it, express love for it, and worship it. And he will find that it will answer him in words, the sentences forming themselves spontaneously within his mind as speech without sound. It will give him pertinent didactic instruction—often at unexpected moments—and formulate higher points of view.

❧

The Overself is there, but it is hidden within our conscious being. Only there, in this deep atmosphere, do we come upon the mirage-free Truth, the illusion-free Reality.

❧

What it asserts is that the real truth already exists in the pithy core of man's mind, that it can be seen by anyone who will undo the illusions which cover it so thickly, the passions which obscure it so agitatedly, and, above all, the egoism which fears it so greatly. This does not imply the development of new things: it implies the removal of old ones. It is concerned with the discovery of what we really are, not what we shall one day become.

❧

. . . every verbal explanation really fails to explain the Overself unless and until we know it for ourself within ourself and as ourself.

❧

The Overself is always present in man's heart. If he does not receive awareness of this fact in his mind, that is because he makes no proper and sustained effort to do so.

❧

Because it is impossible for the questing ego to *become* the Overself, the quester must recognize that he *is* the Overself and stop thinking in egoistic terms of progress along a path, or attainment of a goal.

Is this benign state a past from which we have lapsed or a future to which we are coming? The true answer is that it is neither. This state has always been existent within us, is so now, and always will be. It is forever with us simply because it is what we really are.

The self of every creature is divine Being, the ultimate Consciousness, but only when evolution brings it to the human level does it have the possibility of discovering this fact.

The mineral, the plant, and the animal have the infinite Life-Power within them, too, but they do not know that they have it. Man alone can know his own divinity. . . .

Once you are clearly aware of the presence of the Overself, you will find that it will spontaneously provide you with a rule of conduct and a standard of ethics at all times and under all circumstances. Consequently you will never be at a loss to know what to do in difficult moral situations, nor how to behave in challenging ones. And with this knowledge will also come the power to implement it.

If we believe in or know of the reality of the Overself, we must also believe or know that our everyday, transient life is actively rooted in its timeless being.

❧

When a man discovers that the same Overself dwells in his enemy as in his own heart, how can he ever again bring himself to hate or injure another?

❧

Because he has access to this inward source, he may live the loneliest of lives but it will not be loveless. The joy and warmth of its ever-presence will abide with him.

❧

. . . we must understand that heaven and hell are deep inside the heart and not places to which we go. . . .

❧

It is surprising how widely people have ignored Jesus' message ("The kingdom of heaven is within you") when its meaning is so clear, its phrasing so strong.

Always Here and Now

We live all the time in unfailing, if unconscious, union with the Overself.

❧

How is it that I am—and know that I am—substantially the same man today as yesterday, that I remember the happenings of a year ago? The answer must be that there is a continuous self, or being, or mind, in me, distinct from its thoughts or experiences.

Is it not a strange thing that after a night's dreaming sleep when we may become some other person, some other character during our dreams, we yet wake up with the old identity that we had before the dream? And is it not equally strange that after a night's sweet, deep, dreamless slumber when we actually forget utterly that same previous identity, we are able to pick it up once more on awakening? What is the explanation of these strange facts? It is that we have never left our true selfhood, whether in dreams or deep slumber, never been other than we really were in essence, and that the only change that has taken place has been a change of the *state* of our consciousness, not of the consciousness itself.

The absence of the ego is the presence of the Overself. But this is only a surface impression in the person's thought, for the Overself is *always* present.

The spiritual self, the Overself, has never been lost. What has happened is that its being has not been recognized, covered over as it is with a multitude of thoughts, desires, and egocentricities.

&

What we need to grasp is that although our apprehension of the Real is gradual, the Real is nonetheless with us at every moment in all its radiant totality. Modern science has filled our heads with the false notion that reality is in a state of evolution, whereas it is only our mental concept of reality which is in a state of evolution.

. . . the divine self is always there within him, it is never absent from him, not even for a second. It is the unfailing witness of all his efforts and aspirations. When he has tried hard enough and long enough it will suddenly shed all its Grace upon him.

The Overself is truly our guardian angel, ever with us and never deserting us. It is our invisible saviour. But we must realize that it seeks primarily to save us not from suffering but from the ignorance which is the cause of our suffering.

Let no one imagine that contact with the Overself is a kind of dreamy reverie or pleasant, fanciful state. It is a vital relationship with a current of peace, power, and goodwill flowing endlessly from the invisible centre to the visible self.

Even during the longest dark night of the soul, the Overself is not a whit less close to him than it was when it revealed its presence amid ecstasy and joy.

The Overself is always present but man's attention seldom is.

That which is within us as the Overself, being godlike, is out of time and eternal.

2

The Ego Illusion

There is no permanency anywhere except in ourselves. And even there it is so deep down, and so hard to find, that most people accept the mistaken idea that their ego's ever-changing existence is the only real existence.

To know what his real "I" is not is a first and most important step toward knowing what it really is. Indeed, it has a liberating effect.

Man is like an actor who has become so involved in the interpretation of his role that he has forgotten his original identity. It effectively prevents him from remembering who and what he is.

A Transient Shadow

We draw the very capacity to live from the Overself, the very power to think from the same source. But we confine both the capacity and the power to a small, fragmentary, and mostly physical sphere. Within this confinement the ego sits enthroned, served by our senses and pandered by our thoughts.

The ego's consciousness is a vastly reduced, immeasurably weakened echo of the Overself-Consciousness. It is always changing and dissipates in the end whereas the Other is ever the same and undying. But the ego is drawn out of the Other and must return to it, so the link is there. What is more, the possibility of returning voluntarily and deliberately is also there.

The ego is after all only an idea. It derives its seeming actuality from a higher source. If we make the inner effort to search for its origin we shall eventually find the Mind in which this idea originated. That mind is the Overself. This search is the Quest. The self-separation of the idea from the mind which makes its existence possible, is egoism.

What we commonly think of as constituting the "I" is an idea which changes from year to year. This is the personal "I." But what we feel most intimately as being always present in all these different ideas of the "I," that is, the sense of being, of existence, never changes at all. It is this which is our true enduring "I."

. . . The Overself never descends or climbs, never loses its own sublime consciousness. What really does this is something that emanates from it and that consequently holds its capacity and power in latency, something which is finited out of the Overself's infinitude and becomes first, the simple unit of life and later, the complex human ego. . . .

The thoughts and feelings which flow like a river through our consciousness make up the surface self. But underneath them there is a deeper self which, being an emanation from divine reality, constitutes our true self.

There is no real ego but only a quick succession of thoughts which constitutes the "I" process. There is no separate entity forming the personal consciousness but only a series of impressions, ideas, images revolving round a common centre. The latter is completely empty; the feeling of something being there derives from a totally different plane—that of the Overself.

. . . The personality is but a transient shadow; a shadow presupposes a light; the light of the real self exists; renounce living in the shadow and move over to the light. . . .

As egos they are certainly individual lives and beings. Their separateness is unquestionable. But as manifestations of the One Infinite Life-Power, their separateness from It is a great illusion.

The personal ego of man forms itself out of the impersonal life of the universe like a wave forming itself out of the ocean. It constricts, confines, restricts, and limits that infinite life to a small finite area. The wave does just the same to the water of the ocean. The ego shuts out so much of the power and intelligence contained in the universal being that it seems to belong to an entirely different and utterly inferior order of existence. The wave, too, since it forms itself only on the surface of the water gives no indication in its tiny stature of the tremendous depth and breadth and volume of water beneath it. . . .

With the body, the thoughts, and the emotions, the ego seems to complete itself as an entity. But where do we get this feeling of "I" from? There is only one way to know the answer to this question: the way of meditation. This burrows beneath the three mentioned components and penetrates into the residue, which is found to be nothing in particular, only the sense of Be-ing. And this is the real source of the "I" notion, the self-feeling. Alas! The source does not ordinarily reveal itself, so we live in its projection, the ego, alone. We are content to be little, when we could be great.

If we could pin down this sense of "I"-ness which is behind all we think, say, and do, and if we could part it from the thoughts, feelings, and physical body by doing so, we would find it to be rooted in and linked with the higher Power behind the whole world.

It is not through any intellectual process of reasoning from premise to conclusion that we come to know we exist, but through an immediate and spontaneous intuition.

Even the shell-shocked soldier who suffers from an almost total amnesia, forgetting his personal identity and personal history, does not suffer from any loss of the consciousness that he exists. Its old ideas and images may have temporarily or even permanently vanished, but the mind itself carries on.

Neither deep sleep nor brain concussion prevents us from recovering the sense of "I" when they end.

The ego self is the creature born out of man's own doing and thinking, slowly changing and growing. The Overself is the image of God, perfect, finished, and changeless. What he has to do, if he is to fulfil himself, is to let the one shine through the other.

How shall he know and understand that this very awareness, of which so small is the fragment that he experiences, is a limited and conditioned part of the Great Awareness itself, of God?

What we find as the attributes of the ego are a reflected image, limited and changing, of what we find in the Overself. They ultimately depend on the Overself both for their own existence and their own nature.

Because there is something of God in me as the Overself, god-like qualities and capacities are in me. I am essentially wise, powerful, loving; but to the extent that I identify myself with the little ego, I obscure these grand qualities. . . .

Our attachment to the ego is natural. It arises because we are unconsciously attached to that which is behind it, to the Overself. Only, we are misled by ignorance wholly to concentrate on the apparent "I" and wholly to ignore the unseen, enduring self of which it is but a transient shadow. The "I" which trembles or enjoys in the time-series is not the real "I."

It is ludicrous if that part of the mind which is only within the personal consciousness, the ego, sets itself up to deny the Mind-in-itself—its own very Source. For the ego is shut in what it experiences and knows—a much limited area.

Is it not ironical that the Overself projects the ego so far that it denies its source, and then waits indefinitely for the ego to give itself back?

. . . Is it not logical that when a man's mind is full of his "I" to overflowing, there can be no room for that which transcends it, the Overself?

Keep on thinking about the differences between the personal ego and the impersonal Overself until you become thoroughly familiar with them.

Prisoners of Our Past

. . . In letting ourselves become victims of the past by letting it swallow up the present, we lose the tremendous meaning and tremendous opportunity which the present contains. Whereas the Overself speaks to us from tomorrow's intuitive understanding, the ego speaks to us through memory. Its past enslaves us, preventing a new and higher way of viewing life from being born.

But it is possible to arouse ourselves and to begin viewing life as it unfolds in the Eternal Present, the Now, with wholly fresh eyes. Every morning is like a new reincarnation into this world. It is a fresh chance to be ourselves, not merely echoes of our own past ideological fixations. . . .

This is the ego that we falsely think of as being our real self. This is the ego to which memory ties us. This is the illusive part of our dual personality; this is the known part of our being, a mere shadow thrown by the unknown part which is infinitely greater. This moves from one earthly body to another, from one dream to another through the phantasmagoria of existence without awakening to reality.

We are prisoners of our ego because we are prisoners of our past.

Those who recur often to thoughts of their past get trapped by it and kept prisoner of the ego. Remorse for sins committed and self-pity for being the victim of other people's sinning—both are soon overdone and create more obstacles to be overcome on the quest.

The tendencies and habits, the physical and mental activities which we have brought over from our own past, settle down and congeal themselves into what we call our personal self, our individuality, our ego. Yet life will not permit this combination to be more than a temporary one, and we go on changing with time. We identify ourselves with each of these changes, in turn, yet always think that is really ourself. Only when we still these activities and withdraw from these habits for a brief period in meditation, do we discover for the first time that they do not constitute our real self, after all. Indeed, they are then seen to be our false self, for it is only then that we discover the inner being that is the real self which they hide and cover up. Alas! so strong is their age-old power that we soon allow them to resume their tyrannous ways over us, and we soon become victims again of the great illusion of the ego.

If we succeed in detaching ourselves from the claims of past memories and the anticipations of future results, we succeed in detaching ourselves from the ego. . . .

Whatever helps to lead him out of the ego's tyranny, be it an idea or a situation, an induced mood or a particular service, is worth trying. But it will be easier, and the result more successful, to the extent that he releases himself from his past history.

The ego is a structure which has been built up in former lives from tendencies, habits, and experiences in a particular pattern. But in the end the whole thing is nothing but a thought, albeit a strong and continuing thought.

There comes a time when he has to turn his back on the past, for the old man is becoming a stranger and a new man is coming to birth. Memories would obstruct this process.

The Evolutionary Process

The process of human evolution serves a twofold purpose. The first is to develop the physical, emotional, and intellectual characteristics. The second is to lead the individual to enquire into, and become fully conscious of, his divine origin.

The journey of life is both an adventure and a pilgrimage. We pass from body to body to collect experience. The fruit of experience is Enlightenment: the knowledge of Overself, established awareness of its presence; and knowledge of the Unseen Power behind the universe, established connection with it.

The eventual trend of evolution is through and away from personality, as we now know it. We shall find ourselves afresh in a higher individuality, the soul. To achieve this, the lower characteristics have slowly to be shed. In this sense, we do die to the earthly self and are born again in the higher self. That is the only real death awaiting us.

Man, in his earlier phases of being, was connected with the Overself and aware of it. But his connection lacked his own control. Eventually, to fulfil the purpose of evolution, he lost this connection and with it his awareness. Now he has to regain the connection and reawaken this awareness by his own efforts and out of his own inner activity, through his own desiring and in his own individual freedom. What has he gained by this change to compensate the loss? His consciousness has become more sharply focused and consequently more clearly aware.

Carrying in himself whatever he has found in study and meditation and prayer, he returns to the world to gain experience of life and to apply in practice what he has learned.

Every man is offered a chance to live again, not once but as many times as will bring him to his diviner being and establish him in that. . . .

. . . Is all the vast intelligence of this universe which gave birth to our own minute fragment to be forever separated from us? No! We shall live again, die again, and return again unless and until we have fulfilled the divine purpose which brought us here.

. . . There are two kinds of immortality (so long as the lower self dominates consciousness): first, the "endless" evolution of the ego, gradually developing through all its many manifestations; and, secondly, the true immortality of the everlasting, unchanging Real Self—or Overself—which forever underlies and sustains the former.

Every unfulfilled desire acts as an attractive force to draw us back to earth again after every death.

Every life in the fleshly body represents an opportunity to obtain spiritual realization because man can only discover his divinity to the fullest whilst in the waking state.

It is an irony of life that a man can plainly see the physical ego, but that on which it depends for existence, the Overself, he does not see. Therefore he neglects or ignores the attention it needs and misses much of the opportunity that a reincarnation offers to further his inner unfoldment.

. . . It is not the Overself that suffers and struggles during this long unfoldment but its child, the ego. It is not the Overself that slowly expands its intelligence and consciousness, but the ego. It is not the Overself that gets deluded by ignorance and passion, by selfishness and extroversion, but the ego. . . .

Ironically enough, pain and suffering are not always necessary. But only the few understand this. They may learn quietly from philosophy within a few years what humanity at large must learn brutally through suffering, and relearn again in every epoch.

Our troubles are but transitory, whereas our spiritual hopes survive the incarnations and bridge the gaps between births.

He who has taken many births has a great wealth of total experience behind him. This manifests itself naturally in wiser decisions and better self-control.

Man can come into the personal knowledge that there is this unseen power out of which the whole universe is being derived, including himself. But neither the animal nor the plant can come into this knowledge. Here we see what evolution means and why it is necessary.

No living creature in the kingdom of animals knows more than its immediate surroundings or cares for more than the sustenance of its immediate existence. It lives in an immense and varied universe but that fact is lost to its mentality and outside its interest. Only when the evolving entity attains the stage of developed human beings does this unconsciousness disappear. Then life takes on a larger meaning and the life-force becomes aware of itself, individualized, self-conscious. Only then does a higher purpose become possible and apparent.

. . . what is the use of taking a few small sections of the past, such as childhood or adolescence, and attempting to deal with them only, when the true past of the ego contains innumerable subconscious memories of former lives on earth and numerous tendencies which arise from episodes belonging to that vanished history? . . .

The Body

. . . He must refuse to follow the common error and identify himself with this one physical body of the present incarnation. Rather, he must identify himself with his mental being and feel this as something immortal, something reappearing on earth time after time and coming closer and closer, with each appearance, to the goal. . . .

Life in the flesh is a gift if we are using it rightly but it becomes a curse if we are not. Every incarnation should be used to help one get somewhat farther in doing this job of achieving an Overself-inspired existence.

The man who takes his body for himself, misunderstands himself. Only a course of severe discipline will correct it and reveal to him by intense experience the power subtler than flesh, subtler even than intellect, which is at the vital centre deep within consciousness.

So long as a man identifies himself with the physical body, so long will he perforce have to identify himself with its desires and passions. Only when he transfers this self-identification to the infinite mental being can he completely detach himself from them.

In the human body there is at one and the same time a projection of the Overself and a channel for it. The wisdom and intelligence which have gone into and are hidden behind the whole universe have gone into the human body, too. . . .

Even in the midst of bodily sufferings, he will still keep and not lose this beautiful serenity of mind. And he is able to do so precisely because he is able to differentiate the flesh from the mind. Inevitably, it must counteract, even though it may not obliterate, the body's pain.

. . . To destroy the ego completely would necessarily mean to destroy the physical body, which is a part of it, and to remove his particular individuality which sets him apart from others. This cannot be done, but what can be done is to render the ego subservient to the higher self, an obedient instrument of the higher will.

. . . The ego cannot, indeed, be destroyed so long as we need its services while in the flesh; but it can be subjugated and turned into a servant instead of permitting it to remain a master. . . . The real enemy to be overcome is not the entity ego, but the function of egoism.

You have a body but the real *you* is not physical. You have an intellect but the real you is not intellectual. You have emotions but the real you is not emotional. What then are you? You are the infinite consciousness of the Overself.

Death of the Body

Just when life is ebbing fast away, when death is vividly in attendance, the long-sought but little found state of enlightenment may arise and accompany the event.

Death can open out higher possibilities to the man who leaves this existence in faith, who trusts the Overself and commits himself to its leading without clinging to the body which is being left.

If there is any loss of consciousness during the change called death, it is only a brief one, as brief or briefer than a night's sleep. Many of the departed do not even know at the time what has really happened to them and still believe themselves to be physically alive. For they find themselves apparently able to see others and hear voices and touch things just as before. Yet all these experiences are entirely immaterial, and take place within a conscious mind that has no fleshly brain.

We may deplore our foolish behaviour in life, our stupid errors or our fleshly weaknesses, but in those moments of dying we have the chance to die in wisdom and in peace. Yes, it is a chance given to us, but we have to take it by keeping our sight fixed on the highest that we know.

There is a particular moment while a person is dying when the Overself takes over the entire process, just as it does when he is falling asleep. But if he clings involuntarily and through inveterate habit to his smaller nature, then he is only partly taken over; the remainder is imprisoned in his littleness.

Concealed behind the passing dream of life there is a world of lasting reality. All men awaken at the moment of death but only a few men are able to resist falling at once into the astral dream. These are the few who sought to die to their lower selves whilst they were still alive. These are the mystics who enter reality.

With death, consciousness takes on a new condition but does not pass into mere emptiness, is not crumbled away with the fleshly brain into dust. No! It survives because it is the real being of a man.

We have not come from oblivion. All our past is present in our characters, capacities, and tendencies; therefore we shall not go into oblivion. There is no death—only a change of state.

Dying into annihilation is one thing but dying into another form of consciousness is quite different. It is the latter which happens at the passing away of the life-force from the body.

The entity which lives in the spirit world after death is the same ego that dwelt on earth, emanating from and sustained by the same Overself. In this relationship, they are still distinct and separate entities, even though as intimately connected as parent and offspring.

There are the visible living people and the invisible living ones. None are ever lost to existence or destroyed in consciousness, but only their bodies.

This dream-like progress after death is not valueless. It acts as a reminder during each pre-birth of the true purpose of life.

When the decreed time comes the body is discarded but the mind remains. It passes through varied experiences and finally sleeps them off. After a while it awakes deeply refreshed. Then the old propensities slowly revive and it returns to this world, putting on a new body in new surroundings.

Karma

People should be warned that cause and effect rule in the moral realm no less than in the scientific realm. They should be trained from childhood to take this principle into their calculation. They should be made to feel responsible for setting causes into action that invite suffering or attract trouble or lead to frustration.

He who has sufficiently purified his character, controlled his senses, developed his reason, and unfolded his intuition is always ready to meet what comes and to meet it aright. He need not fear the future. Time is on his side. For he has stopped adding bad karma to his account and every fresh year adds good karma instead. . . .

He who has sufficiently purified his character, controlled his

His moral response to a happening, as also his mental attitude toward it and emotional bearing under it, are largely free. It is in this realm, moreover, that important possibilities of further spiritual growth or else materialistic hardening are available. He may renew inner strength or fall back into sensual weakness.

Men act out of self-interest; but through ignorance of the higher laws, especially that of karma, they may act against that interest.

. . . Each man gets his special set of experiences, which no one else gets. Each life is individual and gets from the law of recompense those which it really needs, not those which someone else needs. The way in which he reacts to the varied pleasant and unpleasant situations which develop in everyday life will be a better index to the understanding he has gained than any mystical visions painted by the imagination.

. . . He knows that each experience which comes to him is what he most needs at the time, even though it be what he likes least. He needs it because it is in part nothing else than his own past thinking, feeling, and doing come back to confront him to enable him to see and study their results in a plain, concrete, unmistakable form. . . .

. . . We must study the lessons behind every experience, painful or pleasant, that karma brings. We lose nothing except what is well worth losing if we frankly acknowledge past errors. Only vanity or selfishness can stand in the way of such acknowledgment. Earthly life is after all a transient means to an enduring end. . . .

Which of us has the power to change the consequences of his former actions? We may make amends, we may be penitent and perform penances. We may counter them by the opposite kinds of good deeds. But it is the business of karma to make us feel responsible for what we do and that responsibility cannot be evaded. In a certain sense, however, there is a measure of freedom, a power of creativity, both of which belong to the godlike Higher Self which each of us has.

The law of consequences is immutable and not whimsical but its effects may at times be modified or even neutralized by introducing new causes in the form of opposing thoughts and deeds. This of course involves in turn a sharp change in the direction of life-course. Such a change we call repentance.

We all have to bear the consequences of our past deeds. This cannot be helped. But of course there are good deeds and bad deeds. We can, to a certain extent, offset those consequences by bringing in counter-forces through new deeds; but how far this will be true will necessarily vary from person to person. The one who has knowledge and power, who is able to practise deep meditation and to control his character, will necessarily affect those consequences much more strongly than the one who lacks these.

. . . Those who understand the principle of karma aright, who do not misunderstand it as being an external independent fate but see it as a force originally set in motion by our actions, understand also the significant part played by suffering in the lives of men. It is educative rather than retributive. . . .

. . . Because the interrelation of outward karma to inner character is so close, he should understand that these difficulties are linked up with his inner state, and that he begins to solve them by removing the imperfection of that inner state. . . .

One shouldn't brood over fancied wrongs which he believes have been done to him nor dwell on another's faults. The law of recompense will deal with the situation. Emotional bitterness is harmful to both persons. On this path, the student must learn to overcome such feelings; they act as obstacles which hinder his advancement.

It is absurd to treat the idea of karma as if it were some outlandish Oriental fancy. It is simply the law which makes each man responsible for his own actions and which puts him into the position of having to accept the results which flow from them. We may call it the law of self-responsibility. . . .

If you want to change your karma, begin by changing your attitude: first, toward outer events, people, things; second toward yourself.

. . . These new ideas will assume the characteristics of seeds, which under the water of the student's own aspiration and the sunshine of visible and invisible forces, will grow gradually into fruitful understanding and deeds. For the karmic consequence of such interest will be one day birth into a family where every opportunity for advancement will be found.

He who has had the good fortune to have a loving companion in marriage should not rail at Destiny when this helpmate is taken away. The same karma which brought the two together has also severed the relationship. But this is only temporary. There is really no loss, as mind speaks to mind in silent moments. Love and companionship of high quality will act as an attractive force to bring them together again somewhere, sometime. Many feel this in the inner understanding.

Life in the Ego

Is it true that most men suffer from mistaken identity? . . .

This is the amazing contradiction of man's life, that although bearing the divine within himself, he is aware only of, and pursues unabated, its very opposite.

What he takes to be his true identity is only a dream that separates him from it. He has become a curious creature which eagerly accepts the confining darkness of the ego's life and turns its back on the blazing light of the soul's life.

So many human sufferings are the consequences of human errors, and so many of these errors arise from human ignorance. The supreme ignorance of all which leads to the greatest sins and sufferings is that he does not know he is an individualized part of a greater consciousness. Although this consciousness shines through his ego it is apart from the ego, for it stands in its own right and exists as an entity by itself. It is this consciousness which enables a man to act and think in the physical body and it is his diviner part. Blinded by the error of materialism, he identifies it with the body itself.

We cannot help living in a human ego or feeling its wishes and desires, for most of us are infatuated with it. But it can be put in its place and kept there, first through a profound understanding, next through a lofty aspiration to transcend it, and third through a following of the Quest until its very end.

Men are locked up within their little egos. They are in prison and do not know it. Consequently they do not ask, much less seek, for freedom.

The unawakened ego submits passively to the lower influences which come to it out of the shadows of its own long past and to the sense-stirring suggestions which come to it out of the surroundings in which it moves. But when it has found and surrendered to the Overself in the heart, this blind, mechanical responsiveness comes to an end and an aroused, enlightened, fully aware, inner rulership replaces it.

We may well wonder how animal lust, human cunning, and angelic nobility can come to be mingled in a single entity. That indeed is the mystery of man.

It is both the irony and tragedy of life that we use up its strictly limited quota of years in pursuits which we come later to see as worthless and in desires which we find bring pain with their fulfilment. The dying man, who sees the cinema-film of his past flash in review before his mental eyes, discovers this irony and feels this tragedy.

The wheel of life keeps turning and turning through diverse kinds of experiences and we are haplessly bound to it. But when at last we gain comprehension of what is happening and power over it, we are set free.

The profound meaning of life is not put before our eyes. We have to dig for it with much patience and much perseverance.

. . . The man of today lives, moves, and has his being in his personal ego and will continue to do so until he has learned, grasped, thoroughly understood, and completely realized the truth of the illusiveness of the individual self. . . .

. . . If he looks only to the little ego for his supply, he must accept all its narrow limitations, its dependence on personal effort alone. But if he looks farther and recognizes his true source of welfare is with the Overself, with its miracle-working Grace, he knows that all things are possible to it. Hope, optimism, and high expectation make his life richer, more abundant.

We are here in this world for a higher purpose than the obvious physical one of self-preservation, for even that is contributory to it. We are here to evolve into the consciousness of Overself. Every physical experience is only a means toward such spiritual development.

The ceaseless longing for personal happiness which exists in every human being is a right one, but is generally mistaken in the direction along which satisfaction is sought. For all outward objects and beings can yield only a transient and imperfect delight that can never be equivalent to the uninterrupted happiness of life in the Overself.

. . . This is the use he is to make of his life on earth: his personal life, his family relations, his professional career—all must become subject to the higher purpose. The resolve made, the matter of success or failure is no longer urgent, for every subsequent embodiment will point in this direction. Philosophy has instructed him in the unreality of time and has revealed to him his indissoluble connection with the Overself. . . .

The key to right conduct is to refuse to identify himself with the lower nature. The hypnotic illusion that it is really himself must be broken: the way to break it is to deny every suggestion that comes from it, to use the will in resisting it, to use the imagination in projecting it as something alien and outside, to use the feelings in aspiration towards the true self, and the mind in learning to understand what it is.

Remember that no enterprise or move should be left to depend on the ego's own limited resources. The humble invocation of help from the Higher Self expands those resources and has a protective value. At the beginning of every day, of every enterprise, of every journey, and of every important piece of work, remember the Overself and, remembering, be obedient to its laws. Seek its inspiration, its power. To make it your silent partner is to double your effectiveness.

. . . When his weaknesses are counterbalanced by earnest aspiration and faith, if he never deserts his Ideal no matter what happens, if he clings to his desire for conscious attainment of unity with the Overself as the highest goal life offers and measures all other rewards accordingly, then the student may always count on the assistance which brought him safely through his time of crisis.

There would be no hope of ever getting out of this ego-centered position if we did not know these three things. First, the ego is only an accumulation of memories and a series of cravings, that is, thought; it is a fictitious entity. Second, the thinking activity can come to an end in stillness. Third, Grace, the radiation of the Power beyond man, is ever-shining and ever-present. If we let the mind become deeply still and deeply observant of the ego's self-preserving instinct, we open the door to Grace, which then lovingly swallows us.

To live in the ego is to live in time, to live in the Overself is to live in timelessness. But because man must live in both to live on earth at all, let him learn the art of resting in the eternal Now, the continuing moment which opens on to eternity.

We murmur against the world's obstructiveness to our aspirations: the body is our stumbling-block. Yet if we had to live always as disembodied spirits, our spiritual development would need an immeasurably longer time to accomplish itself. The sharper focus of physical consciousness quickens our pace.

. . . Even a few years' study of philosophy will bring definite benefit into the life of a student. It will help him in all sorts of ways, unconsciously, here on earth and it will help him very definitely after death during his life in the next world of being.

What if the goal seems too distant or the climb too steep? Do as much or as little as you can to advance. If you lack the strength to go all the way, then go some of the way. Your spiritual longings and labours will influence the nature of your *next* body and the conditions of your next incarnation. Nothing will be lost. Higher capacities and more favourable circumstances will then be yours if you have deserved them. Every virtue deliberately cultivated leads to a pleasanter rebirth. Every weakness remedied leads to the cancellation of an unpleasant one.

Old infirm people who become weary of the body and hence weary of themselves have no way out except the larger identification with something larger than the body self.

❧

There is a deep joy in this growing perception of life's larger meaning, a profound comfort in the ever increasing knowledge of its beneficent purpose.

❧

In first, the discovery of the Overself, and second, the surrender to it, man fulfils the highest purpose of his life on this earth.

3

The Gentle Voice of the Overself

The mystery into which we have been born is not penetrable by weaving fancy or logical intellect. But intuition, if we are patient enough and willing enough to follow it, can lead us into an overwhelming experience where we discover that IT is there, always there.

The promptings that come from this inner being are so faintly heard at first, however strong on their own plane, that we tend to disregard them as trivial. This is the tragedy of man. The voices that so often mislead him into pain-bringing courses—his passion, his ego, and blind intellect—are loud and clamant. The whisper that guides him aright and to God is timid and soft.

In the end he will rely on this little inner voice which, if he listens humbly, speaks and tells him which way to turn.

Intuition Shows the Way

Is he fully open to intuitive feelings that originate in his deeper being, his sacred self? Or does his ego get in the way by its rigidities, habits, and tendencies? The importance of these feelings is that they are threadlike clues which need following up, for they can lead him to a blessed renewal or revelation.

. . . Only through the pure intuition, freed from emotional egoism and transcending intellectual illusion, can he really make a contact with the Overself. And that will happen in a state of utter and perfect tranquillity; there will be none of the emotional excitement which marked the successful practice of the earlier stage of meditation exercises.

. . . Among all the varied powers of the mind, a properly unfolded intuition is indeed one of the most priceless anyone could have. It always warns against wrong courses and often counsels the right ones. . . .

Every thought which comes down to us from that serene height comes with a divine authority and penetrating force which are absent from all other thoughts. We receive the visitant with eagerness and obey it with confidence.

Intuition is not the equal but rather the superior of all other human faculties. It delivers the gentlest of whispers, commands from the Overself, whereas the other faculties merely carry them out. It is the master, they are the servants. The intellect thinks, the will works, and the emotion drives towards the fulfilment of intuitively felt guidance in the properly developed spiritually erect man.

The intuition must lead all the rest of man's faculties. He must follow it even when they do not agree with its guidance. For it sees farther than they ever can, being an efflux from the godlike part of himself which is in its way a portion of the universal deity. If he can be sure that it is not pseudo-intuition, truth in it will lead him to life's best, whether spiritual or worldly.

It is worthwhile giving all his attention to any feelings which he may meet unexpectedly within himself and which show an unusual relaxation, a release from tenseness, a freedom from care. They are to be caught on the wing, not allowed to escape and pass away. They are to be nurtured, cherished, and developed. They may be silent voices from the higher self drawing his attention to its own existence.

Intuitions move in on us in one of two ways: either so soft and gentle at first as almost to be missed or with such aggressive forcefulness as to allow no other way.

What is more private, more intimate, than intuition? It is the only means they possess wherefrom to start to get mystical experience, glimpses, true enlightenment. Yet they insist on seeking among those who stand outside them, among the teachers, for that which must be searched after and felt inside themselves.

From the outside, by means of events, persons, or books; from the inside, by means of intuitions, thoughts, feelings, and urges—this is how the way is shown him by the Overself.

An intuitive idea is quite different from one derived from the customary process of logical thinking. Unless it is distorted or muddled by the man himself, it is always reliable. Can we say the same of an intellectual idea?

The intellect has so dominated the modern man that his approach to these questions is first made through it. Yet the intellect cannot provide the answers to them. They come, and can only come, through the intuition.

Logical thinking about a proposed course can never be equal to intuitive guidance about it. For the first is limited by the ego's capacity and experience whereas the second transcends them.

The unregarded feeling which first comes when an object, a person, or an event confronts one is mostly the correct intuition about it. But it must be caught on the wing or it will be gone.

The constant movement of thoughts and the ego's fascination with itself hide from us the divine Overself, from which both are derived.

The discovery of its presence makes possible a form of communication between person and Overself which is passive, not active. That is, he is directed guided or corrected in and through his human faculties, intuitively. The person acts, does, thinks, speaks, and decides as if he were doing so completely alone. But he is not: he is responding to the Overself, to the effects of its presence, now unhindered by his ego.

If only he heeds its intuitive message, the higher self will not fail him. He will make his way to true balanced sanity and deep inner calm. Without searching for others, knowing that in himself God's representative resides and that this can give the right kind of help, he will depend for self-reliance on an ever-presence.

There is no single pattern that an intuitively guided life must follow. Sometimes he will see in a flash of insight both course and destination, but at other times he will see only the next step ahead and will have to keep an open mind both as to the second step and as to the final destination.

When a man hesitates too long over taking a course which intuition tells him he should take, and in which his higher life is concerned, it may be that destiny will intervene and make him suddenly realize that this *is* the way, and that all doubts should be thrown out.

It is the strength or feebleness of our intuition which determines the grade of our spiritual evolution. What begins as a gentle surrender to intuition for a few minutes, one day resolves into a complete surrender of the ego to the Overself for all time.

Take Time to Listen

Treasure every moment when the intuition makes itself felt and, most especially, when it takes the form of a glimpse into higher truth; it is then that other things should be well put aside in order to sustain and prolong the experience.

There is a faculty in man which knows truth when it sees it, which needs no argument, reflection, or cogitation to attest or prove what it knows.

Intuition is the voice which is constantly calling him to this higher state. But if he seldom or never pauses amid the press of activity to listen for it, he fails to benefit by it.

Whatever be the personal problem, if reason, experience, and authority cannot solve it, carry it inwards to the deep still centre. But you must learn to wait in patience for the answer, for the blockage is in you, not in it. A day or a month may pass until the response is felt, thought, or materialized.

We blunder in life and make endless mistakes because we have no time to listen for the Overself's voice—Intuition.

It is one secret of the inspired individual that he *lets* himself be led: he does not try to do with his ego what can be better done for him by the intuition. But this will be possible only if he pauses and waits for the inner leading to come to him.

The man who has trained himself to listen for the voice of intuition, which means trained himself to wait for it to speak and disciplined himself to be inwardly alert yet also inwardly quiet for it, does not have to suffer the painful conflicts and tormenting divisions which others do when confronted by issues demanding a choice or a decision.

Intuitive guidance comes not necessarily when we seek it, but when the occasion calls for it. It does not usually come until it is actually needed. The intellect, as part of the ego, will often seek it in advance of the occasion because it may be driven by anxiety, fear, desire, or anticipation. Such premature seeking is fruitless.

If he can come to this belief in the reality of his own higher self, he can come into all the knowledge he needs, all the help he needs, by heeding its guidance (felt intuitively) and by applying its injunctions to his daily life.

The need to guide his personal life more intuitively comes home to him after every major mistake has been committed and its effects felt. He sees then that it is not enough to calculate by intellect, nor feel by impulse, nor act on emotion, for these have led him to sufferings that could have been prevented, or caused other people sufferings that bring him regrets. He learns that it is necessary to listen inwardly, to wait in mental quiet for intuitive feeling to arise and guide him.

Once you learn to recognize the intuitive voice, follow its dictates; do not hesitate to conform with them or try to make up an excuse for failing to do so if the guidance is unpalatable.

In trying to get an intuitive answer, it is important to formulate the problem or the questions clearly and as sharply as you can.

Intuition tells us *what* to do. Reason tells us *how* to do it. Intuition points direction and gives destination. Reason shows a map of the way there.

You may recognize the voice of wisdom when having to make a decision by the fact that it proceeds out of deep inner calm, out of utter tranquillity, whereas impulse is frequently born in exaggerated enthusiasm or undue excitement.

The Overself issues its commands and exacts its demands in the utter silence and privacy of a man's heart. Yet they are more powerful and more imperious in the end than any which issue from the noisy bustling world.

A man's life will be less troubled and his happiness more secured, if his reason governs his body and his intuition governs his reason.

He may be sure of this, that whatever action the Overself's leading causes him to take will always be for his ultimate good even though it may be to his immediate and apparent detriment.

Ordinarily, ample time is needed to accumulate data and deliberate properly before correct decisions or judgements can be made. None of this is necessary to make them intuitively, for the intuition itself operates out of time and beyond thought.

Submit yourself as an empty vessel to be filled with the intuitive leading of Overself. Do not stop short of this goal, do not be satisfied with a half-and-half sort of life.

A man is really free when his intuition directs his intellect and rules his energies.

Ego Impulse or Real Intuition

No counsel could be safer and better than that which proceeds from a man to himself by way of intuition. But first let him be sure that it *is* intuition.

How can he tell if inner guidance is truly intuitive or merely pseudo-intuitive? One of the ways is to consider whether it tends to the benefit of all concerned in a situation, the others as well as oneself. The word "benefit" here must be understood in a large way, must include the spiritual result along with the material one. If the guidance does not yield this result, it may be ego-prompted and will then hold the possibility of error.

. . . The difference between a mere impulse and a real intuition may often be detected in two ways: first, by waiting a few days, as the subconscious mind has then a chance to offer help in deciding the matter; second, by noting the kind of emotion which accompanies the message. If the emotion is of the lower kind, such as anger, indignation, greed, or lust, it is most likely an impulse. If of the higher kind, such as unselfishness or forgiveness, it is most likely an intuition.

An intuition comes into the mind suddenly. But so does an impulse. Therefore it is not enough to take this mark alone to identify it. It is strong; so is an impulse. It is clear; so is an impulse. To separate the deceptive appearance from the genuine reality of an intuition, look for the trail of assurance, relief, and peace to follow in its wake.

. . . Until, therefore, his development has reached the point where a genuine intuition is at once recognized as such and a pseudo-intuition quickly detected for what it is, he must not abandon the use of reason but rather regard it as a most valuable ally.

The day will come when constant effort and long practice will permit him to recognize true from pseudo-intuition with the speed and certainty with which a musically trained ear recognizes notes and times (tunes) in a played piece.

If it is authentic intuition, he will feel increasingly convinced by it as days and weeks pass until in the end its truth will seem unarguable to him.

Cultivate Your Intuitive Sensitivity

The power to commune with the Overself is within us all, but most do not trouble to exert themselves in the nurture and cultivation of it. Hence they do not possess it in actuality.

His first step is to detect the presence of the higher Power consciously in himself through vigilantly noting and cultivating the intuitions it gives him.

He has to train himself to catch what the soul intuits as clearly as he can already catch what the intellect thinks and the body reports.

If you can attentively trace this subtle feeling back to its own root, you will get a reward immeasurably greater than it seemed to promise.

The secret is to stop, on the instant, whatever he is doing just then, or even whatever he is saying, and reorient all his attention to the incoming intuition. . . .

The interval between the coming and the going of an intuitive thought is so short that he must immediately and alertly respond to it. If he misses it, he will find that the mind can go back to it only with difficulty and uncertainty.

To find your way to the major truths it is not enough to use the intellect alone, however sharpened it may be. Join intuition to it: then you will have intelligence. But how does one unfold intuition? By penetrating deeper and hushing the noise of thoughts.

. . . The practice of meditation is simply the deepening, broadening, and strengthening of intuition. A mystical experience is simply a prolonged intuition.

To *let* the intuitive feelings come through requires an inner passivity which meditation fosters but which extroversion inhibits.

Feeling is as much a part of true insight into the Real as knowing. It gives life to the end result. It is evoked by enlightened writings and inspired art works. Thinking may not rightly claim overlordship here, but intuition, the silent voice of the Overself, may do so.

It is needful to bring oneself to abstain from all actions for a short time daily, and to let thinking and feeling slip little by little into complete repose. As the movements of the body are suspended and the workings of the mind are reduced, the rest afforded both of them opens a way for the presence of intuition to be detected, recognized, and connected with. The ego begins to get out of the way, giving what is behind it a chance to reveal itself and be heard.

When the brain is too active, its energies obstruct the gentle influx of intuitive feeling. When they are extroverted, they obstruct that listening attitude which is needed to hear the Overself's gentle voice speak to the inner silence. Mental quiet must be the goal. We must develop a new kind of hearing.

The giving up of all earthly desires, the liberation of the heart from all animal passions, the letting go of all egoistic grasping —these attitudes will arise spontaneously and grow naturally if a man is truly quest-minded, so that his intuition will assert itself little by little.

What is the use of educating so many young people's heads when we leave their intuitive natures absolutely untouched, uncultivated, and unused?

The capacity for intuition is born from a long experience in bygone lives but the psychological reality of it was always present —because the Overself was.

To complain that you get no answer, no result from going into the silence indicates two things: first, that you do not go far enough into it to reach the intuitive level; second, that you do not wait long enough for it to affect you.

The commonest error is to try to produce and manufacture intuition. That can't be done. It is something which comes to you. Hence don't expect it to appear when concentrating on a problem, but if at all *after* you've dismissed the problem. Even then it is a matter of grace—it may or may not come.

The Overself may use some event, some person, or some book as a messenger to him. It may make any new circumstance act in the same way. But he must have the capacity to recognize what is happening and the willingness to receive the message.

When we keep ourselves busy with everything external and our minds with thoughts about everything external, the intuition is unable to insert itself into our awareness. Even if it whispers to us, we will not realize what is happening. If we continue to ignore it, we may lose the capacity to hear it at all. It is then that we have to retrain ourselves to do so. The practice of meditation is one such way of training our receptivity.

If he feels the intuition but does not attend to it then, however slightly, the very faculty which produced it begins to lose strength. This is the penalty imposed for the failure, and this shows how serious it is.

Here is this wonderful potency in man lying largely unused, this faculty of intuition that links him with a higher order of being.

4

Foretaste of the Ego-free Life

It is a state of exquisite tenderness, of love welling up from an inner centre and radiating outward in all directions. If other human beings or animal creatures come within his contact at the time, they become recipients of this love without exception. For then no enemies are recognized, none are disliked, and it is not possible to regard anyone as repulsive.

These brief flashes bring with them great joy, great beauty, and great uplift. They are, for most people, their first clear vivid awakening to the existence and reality of a spiritual order of being. The contrast with their ordinary state is so tremendous as to shame it into pitiful drabness. . . .

Once he has experienced the glimpse he will understand why his next goal is to experience it again, and why his final goal is to attain it in permanence.

An Unforgettable Experience

The revelation wells up slowly, quietly, deeply; it is unfaltering and continues so long as he does not interrupt or interfere with it by his own thoughts. It is really his own innermost guide and guru, his higher self.

However dark or blundering the past, however miserable the tangle one has made of one's life, this unutterable peace blots it all out. Within that seraphic embrace error cannot be known, misery cannot be felt, sin cannot be remembered. A great cleansing comes over the heart and mind.

They may come quite abruptly, those intensely lived moments of true vision, those spasmodic glimpses of a beauty and truth above the best which earthly life offers. The mind then rests and there is a gap in its usual activities, a Void out of which these heavenly experiences come to life as they overcome our ordinary feelings.

You will comprehend that while the Overself thus enfolds you, you can never again feel lonely, never again find the sky turned black because some human love has been denied or been withdrawn from you.

In those moments when he touches the still centre of his being, he forgets his miseries and enjoys its happiness. This provides a clue to the correct way to find real happiness, which so many are seeking and so few are finding. It lies within.

With the glimpse there comes a curious feeling of absolute certitude, happy certitude, utter doubtlessness. The truth *is* there plainly before him and deeply sensed within him.

It is not only the hidden and mysterious source of their own little self but also the unrecognized source of the only moments of real happiness that they ever have.

The Glimpse comes as a benediction and as a grace. The heart should be grateful, immensely grateful for its visitation. It possesses a beauty which is not of this world, which gives joy to the heart.

In these moments of a glimpse, he discovers the very real presence of the Overself. They provide him with a joy, an amiability, which disarms the negative side of his character and brings forward the positive side. These are precious moments; they cannot be too highly valued. And though they must pass, some communication with them is always possible through memory.

❦

Because it gives new hope, fresh encouragement, and the prospect of eventual relief from trouble, the glimpse is like a rainbow in the sky. It reminds him that a providential love is still behind the world and his own existence.

The early Christians who spoke of being "in Christ" were men whose intense faith, devotion, and sacrifice had lifted them into the Overself consciousness.

Only by a personal discovery of the soul, and consequently only by going "inside" himself to discover it, can a man know himself.

It is not by any kind of privilege that anyone obtains the glimpse but by preparation and equilibration, with some amount of purification. To equilibrate is to calm feelings as and when necessary and render them deeper, exquisitely delicate.

These glimpses will last longer and come more easily, hence more often, if the mind and the feelings are properly balanced, and if, at the same time, the body is purified, its organs co-operated with, and its forces regenerated.

It should be remembered that whatever kind of meditation is adopted, the glimpse which comes from it comes because we have provided the right condition for its appearance, not because our own doing makes the glimpse appear. For it comes from the realm of timelessness with which we come into some sort of harmony through the intuitive nature. What we do is in the realm of time, and it can only produce effects of a like nature.

It is never present without certain qualities being present with it, too. There is first an utter serenity, then a steady joy, next an absolute conviction of its truth and reality, finally the paradoxical feeling of a rock-firm security despite any appearance of adverse outer circumstances.

The concentration upon the glimpse must be full, complete, and sustained. If, for only a single moment, he allows his attention to be diverted toward some outer thing or person, or to be divided with some inner idea, the glimpse may instantly disappear.

Those who have followed the Quest in previous lives will generally receive a glimpse at least twice during the present one. They will receive it in early life during their teens or around the threshold of adult life. This will inspire them to seek anew. They will receive it again in late life during the closing years of the reincarnation. This will be bestowed as a Grace of the Overself. . . .

Confirmation and Evidence

The experience tells him vividly, luminously, and memorably that there is an existence beyond the physical one and a consciousness beyond the personal one.

With a glimpse comes revelation. He feels that he belongs to an immortal race, that there is an inner Reality behind all things, and that the ultimate source is a beneficent one.

The Glimpse provides assurance that the Soul exists, that God is, that the purpose of human life must include spiritual fulfilment to be complete. . . .

The divine self reveals itself for a few thrilling moments and then draws back into the void where it dwells. But the glimpse is enough to tell him that a higher kind of life is possible and that there is a being beyond the ego.

When one is allowed a glimpse of the World-Idea, he feels that he understands at last why he came here, what he has to do, and where his place is. It is like an immense enlargement of the mind, an escape from the littleness of the ego, and a finding-out of a long-hidden secret.

A single glimpse will offer all the evidence his reason needs, all the proof his judgement demands that there is a kingdom of heaven and that it is the best of all things to search for.

The Glimpse provides overwhelming confirmation of the belief in a divine principle, positive certainty that it rules the world, and renewed assurance that one day all men will obey its benign prompting towards goodness and wisdom.

The glimpse gives a man either a revelation or a confirmation that something exists which transcends this ordinary life, that it is holy, beautiful, satisfying, and that he may commune with it.

The experience explains a man to himself for the first time, lights up the fact that he lives in two planes at one and the same time. It reveals his ego as the illusion which envelops his consciousness and his Overself as the reality behind his consciousness.

The glimpse is impermanent, its satisfactions fugitive; but it leaves behind a residue of hope and revelation which the impermanent and fugitive pleasures of the world can never do.

It is in those uplifted moments that one has the possibility of coming near to confirm the Pythagorean belief that the human soul is an emanation of the Universal Divine Mind.

What are the signs whereby he shall know that this is an authentic glimpse of reality? First, it is and shall remain ever present. There is no future in it and no past. Second, the pure spiritual experience comes without excitement, is reported without exaggeration, and needs no external authority to authenticate it.

Although it is not possible to offer irrefutable scientific proof of the doctrine of spiritual evolution, it can be shown to be as reasonable a doctrine as any of its rivals. And for those who have had mystical experience of the divine presence behind the mind, of divine wisdom behind the cosmos, it is the only acceptable doctrine.

Psychologists and psychoanalysts are beginning to find a minority among their ranks who put a high value upon these glimpses which they call "peak-experiences." Academically qualified, professionally trained, and science-oriented just like their colleagues, they yet differ in appreciating and studying such experiences as being important to an adequate knowledge of the human being.

We cannot attain reality, for we already are in it; but we can attain consciousness of it. And such consciousness arises naturally the moment we know appearance as being appearance. This knowledge may be nothing more than a second's glimpse, before old habit powerfully reasserts itself again, but it will be enough to tell us the truth.

Many people pass through these experiences of the glimpse and do not really know what is happening to them because they have never studied or been taught anything about such experiences.

He may have to weep for a mere glimpse of the soul. But this got, he will certainly weep again for its return. For he knows now by unshakeable conviction and by this vivid demonstration that the durable realization of the Soul is what he is here on earth for.

It is always possible for a man to gain enlightenment anytime anywhere even though it may not be probable, for he has within himself the Light itself as an ever-present Reality. What does happen and what is probable is that some moment during the course of a lifetime a glimpse may happen, and the glimpse itself is nothing less than a testimony to that ever-presence, a witness telling him that it is true and real.

These glimpses are only occasional. They take us unawares and depart from us unexpectedly. But the joy they bring with them, the insight they bestow, make us yearn for a permanent and unbroken attainment of the state they tell us about.

Too soon he will find that the rebirth was not a durable spiritual event but a temporary one. It offered a picture of something for which, from then on, he must start working in earnest. It was a glimpse only but it provided testimony, evidence, confirmation.

The passing from hope to certainty comes with the glimpse.

Waiting for Liberation

Only those who have felt it can know the completely satisfying nature of the love which flows to and fro between the ego and the Overself at such enkindled moments. They may be gone the same day but they will reflect themselves in a whole lifetime's aspiration thereafter.

During the glimpse he left himself and found a being within which transcended it. After the glimpse he has the chance to create a conscious relationship between them. His outer life ought to carry the mark of this extraordinary event.

He returns from his first initiation into the egoless life with a rich cargo. He carries the stability of peace. A strange feeling of safety takes possession of him at that time. He knows neither care for the uncertain future nor regret for the unpleasant past. He knows that henceforth the life of his being is in the hands of the higher self, and with this he is quite content.

The glimpse is a memorable experience, but it is not enough. It shows him a possible future, gives him a new world-view, but he must henceforth bring all that into his everyday life and into his whole being. This needs time, practice, patience, vigilance, self-training, and more sensitivity.

. . . By that glimpse he will have been uplifted to a new dimension of being. The difficulty will consist in retaining the new perception. For ancient habits of erroneous thinking will quickly reassert themselves and overwhelm him enough to push it into the background. This is why repeated introspection, reflective study, and mystical meditation are needed to weaken those habits and generate the inner strength which can firmly hold the higher outlook against these aggressive intruders from his own past.

The contemplation in memory of those glimpses will help him to weaken the power of negative thoughts and to weaken, however slightly, the very source of those thoughts, the ego.

He who has tasted the immeasurable joy of the Overself's peace will not care to shrink back again into the little self's confines. For he will know then that the Infinite, the Void, the Transcendent—call what he will the loss of his ego—is not a loss of happiness but an unlimited magnification of it.

If he once has an experience of his divine soul he should remember that this was because it is always there, always inside of him, and has never left him. Let him but stick to the Quest, and the experience will recur at the proper time.

It is objected, why search at all if one really is the Overself? Yes, there comes a time when the deliberate purposeful search for the Overself has to be abandoned for this reason. Paradoxically, it is given up many times, whenever he has a Glimpse, for at such moments he knows that he always was, is, and will be the Real, that there is nothing new to be gained or searched for. . . .

What, it has been asked, if I get no glimpses? What can I do to break this barren, monotonous, dreary, and sterile spiritual desert of my existence? The answer is if you cannot meditate successfully go to nature, where she is quiet or beautiful; go to art where it is majestic, exalting; go to hear some great soul speak, whether in private talk or public address; go to literature, find a great inspired book written by someone who has had the glimpses.

The glimpse is to be welcomed as a relief from the unsatisfactory limitations of ordinary existence. But because it gives enlighten-ment only temporarily, it is not enough. It is necessary to seek out the way of getting a permanent result. . . .

The isolated glimpses will have this effect, that they will not only whet his appetite for farther ones but also for a lasting identity with the Overself.

. . . the philosophical seeker incessantly returns to its remem-brance, uses it to work continuously at the transformation of his self and never lets go of the vision.

⟋

. . . One day the mysterious event called by Jesus being "born again" will occur. There will be a serene displacement of the lower self by the higher one. It will come in the secrecy of the disciple's heart and it will come with an overwhelming power which the intellect, the ego, and the animal in him may resist, but resist in vain. . . .

⟋

A continuous insight, present all the time, is the goal, not a passing glimpse.

⟋

In each of these glimpses, his quest attains a minor climax, for each is a step towards full illumination.

⟋

If it soon fades away, it is a glimpse. If he can stay in it every minute of his waking life, it is illumination.

5

Born Again

. . . This is what I found: The ego vanished; the everyday "I" which the world knew and which knew the world, was no longer there. But a new and diviner individuality appeared in its place, a consciousness which could say "I AM" and which I recognized to have been my real self all along. It was not lost, merged, or dissolved: it was fully and vividly conscious that it was a point *in* universal Mind and so not apart from that Mind itself. Only the lower self, the false self, was gone but that was a loss for which to be immeasurably grateful.

The body seems far away, but *I* seem closer than ever. For I feel that now I am in my mind and no longer the body's captive. There is a sense of release. I am as free as Space itself.

. . . I am conscious of the truth, for I have been lifted like a babe out of all anxiety for the future, all regret for the past. In the spiritual self, I feel a timeless life: I breathe the calm air of the Eternal. I feel safe and I could not worry even if I wanted to. . . .

The Awakening

. . . There will come suddenly unexpectedly and in the dead of night, as it were, a tremendous Realization of the egoless state, a tremendous feeling of liberation from itself as it has known itself, a tremendous awareness of the infinitude, universality, and intelligence of life. . . .

❧

This is the spiritual climax of one's life, this dramatic moment when consciousness comes to recognize and understand itself.

❧

Desires die of themselves without struggle, karma comes to an end, the stillness of the Overself settles in him.

❧

To enter into Heaven is to enter into the fulfilment of our earthly life's unearthly purpose. And that is, simply, to become aware of the Overself. This holy awareness brings such joy with it that we then know why the true saints and the real ascetics were able to disdain all other joys. The contrast is too disproportionate. Nothing that the world offers to tempt us can be put on the same level.

❧

All metaphysical study and all mystical exercises are but preparations for this flash of reality across the sky of consciousness which is here termed insight. The latter is therefore the most important experience which awaits a human being on this earth. . . .

. . . the actual finding of Truth, which is the same as Nirvana, Self-Knowledge, Liberation, is really a work of brief duration—perhaps a matter of minutes—whereas the preparation and equipment of oneself to find it must take many incarnations. . . .

He sees the truth as with a jolt. There it is, within his own being, lying deep down but still in his own self. There never was any need to travel anywhere to find it; no need to visit anyone who was supposed to have it already, and sit at his feet; not even to read any book, however sacred or inspired. Nor could another person, place, or writing give it to him—he would have to unveil it for himself in himself. The others could direct him to look inwards, thus saving all the effort of looking elsewhere. But he himself would have to give the needful attention to himself. The discovery must be his own, made within the still centre of his being.

The discovery of his true being is not outwardly dramatic, and for a long time no one may know of it, except himself. The world may not honour him for it: he may die as obscure as he lived. But the purpose of his life has been fulfilled; and God's will has been done.

No announcements tell the world that he has come into enlightenment. No heralds blow the trumpets proclaiming man's greatest victory—over himself. This is in fact the quietest moment of his whole life.

❧

The Overself is not a goal to be attained but a realization of what already is. It is the inalienable possession of all conscious beings and not of a mere few. No effort is needed to get hold of the Overself, but every effort is needed to get rid of the many impediments to its recognition. We cannot take hold of it; it takes hold of us. Therefore the last stage of this quest is an effortless one. We are led, as children by the hand, into the resplendent presence. Our weary strivings come to an abrupt end. Our lips are made shut and wordless.

❧

The mind must go on gradually parting with its ancient illusions, its time-fed prejudices, hardly aware of any progress, until one fateful day truth triumphs abruptly in a vivid flash of supreme illumination.

❧

The passing over into higher consciousness cannot be attained by the will of any man, yet it cannot be attained without the will of man. Both grace and effort are needed.

❧

When he has silenced his desires and stilled his thoughts, when he has put his own will aside and his own ego down, he becomes a free channel through which the Divine Mind may flow into his own consciousness. No evil feelings can enter his heart, no evil thoughts can cross his mind, and not even the new consequence of old wrong-doing can affect his serenity.

As the two interact—the human purpose and the World-Idea—each man slowly unfolds his intelligence, which is the fusion of intellect with intuition, and this culminates in Enlightenment, the ultimate and revelatory Insight.

The Sage

The sage is a man who lives in constant truth-remembrance. He has realized the existence of the Overself, he knows that he partakes of Its life, immortal and infinite. He has made the pilgrimage to essential being and returned again to walk amongst men, to speak their language, and to bear witness, by his life amongst them, to Truth.

. . . mental peace is a fruit of the first and lowest degree of illumination, although thoughts will continue to arise although gently, and thinking in the discursive manner will continue to be active although slowly. But concentration will be sufficiently strong to detach him from the world and, as a consequence, to yield the happiness which accompanies such detachment. . . .

In the moment that there dawns on his understanding the fact of Mind's beginninglessness and deathlessness, he gains the second illumination, the first being that of the ego's illusoriness and transiency.

❧

In the early stages of enlightenment, the aspirant is overwhelmed by his discovery that God is within himself. It stirs his intensest feelings and excites his deepest thoughts. But, though he does not know it, those very feelings and thoughts still form part of his ego, albeit the highest part. So he still separates his being into two—self and Overself. Only in the later stages does he find that God not only is within himself but is himself.

❧

The highest attainment in philosophy, that of the sage, comes from a union of the sharpest, subtlest thinking and the capacity to enter the thought-free state—a combination of real knowledge and felt peace—balanced, united, yielding truth. This is what makes the sage, whose understanding and peace are his own, who does not depend upon any outside person. Yet it is not the little ego's emotion nor its intellectuality which has brought him to this truth. It is the highest human mind, the finest human feeling. The total man cannot lose what he has attained. It is the higher power working inside the human being.

❧

. . . those who have developed insight perceive the essential stuff of everything even while they perceive its forms; hence they see all as *One*. It is as if a dreamer were to know that he was dreaming and thus understand that all the dream scenes and figures were nothing but one and the same stuff—his mind—while not losing his dream experience.

The man who has this higher consciousness permanently will see and experience the outer world like other men, but he will understand the relation between what he sees and the Real world which is behind it. . . .

To arrive at a simultaneous consciousness of both states—the personal ego and the impersonal Overself—is possible, and has been done intermittently by some people such as mystics and artists—or permanently by philosophers.

There are two kinds of consciousness, one is in ever-passing moments, the other ever-present. The one is in time, the other out of it. The ordinary person knows only the one; the enlightened sage knows both.

There is a part of himself which cannot die, cannot pass into annihilation. But it is very deep down. The sage encounters it before bodily death and learns to establish his consciousness therein. The others encounter it during some phase in the after-death state.

Whereas every human personality is different in its characteristics from every other one, no human Overself is different in its characteristics from any other one. The seekers of all times and all places have always found one and the same divine being when they found the Overself.

It is a matter of complete assurance and scientific observation for the sage that God exists, that man has a soul, that he is here on earth to become united with this soul, and that he can attain true happiness only by following good and avoiding evil.

To do something really worthwhile, to become creative and constructive in an inspired way, aware of the Overself, is to become godlike. We then fulfil the purpose of human existence on earth.

. . . It is impossible for the materialist to perceive that we live and move and have our being in a universal Mind. But the sage, knowing this, knows also that this universal life will take care of his individual life to the degree that he opens himself out to it, to the extent that he takes a large and generous view of his relation to all other individual lives.

He who has discovered how to live with his higher self has discovered a serenity which defies circumstance and environment, a goodness which is too deep for the world's understanding, a wisdom which transcends thought.

The man who is established in the Overself cannot be deflected from the calm which it gives into passions, angers, hatreds, and similar base things. Calmness has become his natural attitude.

He who attains this beautiful serenity is absolved from the misery of frustrated desires, is healed of the wounds of bitter memories, is liberated from the burden of earthly struggles. He has created a secret, invulnerable centre within himself, a garden of the spirit which neither the world's hurts nor the world's joys can touch. . . .

He who finds the Overself, loses the burdens, the miseries, and the fears of the ego.

Pain and suffering belong only to this physical world and its shadow-spheres. There is a higher world, where joy and happiness alone are man's experience.

When this contact with the Overself is established, its power will work for you: you will no longer go through the struggles of life alone.

He finds that having attained this liberation of his will from the ego's domination, his freedom has travelled so far that it loses itself and ceases to be free. For it vanishes into the rule of his higher self, which takes possession of him with a completeness and a fullness that utterly hoop him around. Henceforth, its truth is his truth, its goodness is his goodness, and its guidance his obedience.

When the ego is displaced and the Overself is using him, there will be no need and no freedom to choose between two alternatives in regard to actions. Only a single course will present itself, directly and unwaveringly, as the right one.

His thoughts are guided by the Overself, his emotions inspired by it, and his actions expressive of it. Thus his whole personal life becomes a harmoniously and divinely integrated one.

For the man in that high consciousness and identified with it, the ego is simply an open channel through which his being may flow into the world of time and space. It is not himself, as it is for the unenlightened man, but an adjunct to himself, obeying and expressing his will.

The effects of enlightenment include: an imperturbable detachment from outer possessions, rank, honours, and persons; an overwhelming certainty about truth; a carefree, heavenly peace above all disturbances and vicissitudes; an acceptance of the general rightness of the universal situation, with each entity and each event playing its role; and impeccable sincerity which says what it means, means what it says.

Man will be redeemed and saved. This is not mere pious wishful thinking but ineluctable destiny. The divine World-Idea could not be realized if this redemption and this salvation were not eventually possible and inescapably certain.

There are individuals scattered here and there who have found the Overself. . . . it is certain that the whole race will also one day find the Overself.

He who has attuned himself to the egoless life and pledged himself to the altruistic life will find that in abandoning the selfish motives which prompt men he has lost nothing after all. For whatever he really needs and whenever he really needs it, it will come to his hands. And this will be equally true whether it be something for himself or for fulfilment of that service to which he is dedicated. Hence a Persian scripture says: "When thou reachest this station [the abandonment of all mortal attachments], all that is thy highest wish shall be realized."

Whoever has attained this blessed state would not be true to himself if he were not ardently happy to share it with others, if he were not ever ready to help them attain it too. And this desire extends universally to all without exception. He excludes none. . . .

The noble and beautiful teachings of old Greece, from the Socratic to the Stoic, harmonize perfectly with the age-old teachings of the higher philosophy. Although they taught a lofty self-reliance they did not teach a narrow self-centeredness. This is symbolized vividly in Plato's story of the cave, where the man who attained Light immediately forsook his deserved rest to descend to the help and guidance of the prisoners still living in the cave's darkness.

The adept is happy indeed when a student comes into the full realization of the Kingdom of Heaven, for whoever finds it, naturally wants to share it with others.

6

The Inner Voyage

The very idea of a quest involves a passage, a definite movement from one place to another. Here, of course, the passage is really from one state to another. It is a holy journey, so he who is engaged on it is truly a pilgrim. And as on many journeys, difficulties, fatigues, obstacles, delays, and allurements may be encountered on the way, yes! And here there will certainly be dangers, pitfalls, oppositions, and enmities too. His intuition and reason, his books and friends, his experience and earnestness will constitute themselves as his guide upon it. There is another special feature to be noted about it. It is a homeward journey. The Father is waiting for his child. The Father will receive, feed, and bless him.

There is nothing more important in life than the Quest, and the time will come when the student discovers that there is nothing more enjoyable as well. This is inevitable in a Quest whose essential nature is one of infinite harmony and unbroken peace. No worldly object, person, or pleasure can ever bestow the satisfaction experienced in uniting with the Overself.

The goal is to obtain a higher consciousness which flashes across the mind with blinding light. All his effort, all his training is really for this.

The Spiritual Quest

Man's need is twofold: recollection of his divine nature and redemption from his earthly nature.

Love of the Overself is the swiftest horse that can bear us to the heavenly destination. For the more we love It, the less we love the ego and its ways.

The first duty of man, which takes precedence over all other duties, is to become conscious of his Overself. This is the highest duty and every other duty must bow before it. . . .

What or who is seeking enlightenment? It cannot be the higher Self, for that is itself of the nature of Light. There then only remains the ego! This ego, the object of so many denunciations and denigrations, is the being that, transformed, will win truth and find Reality even though it must surrender itself utterly in the end as the price to be paid.

The highest goal of the quest is not illumination gained by destruction of the ego but rather by perfection of the ego. It is the function of egoism which is to be destroyed, not that which functions. The ego's rulership is to go, not the ego itself.

His part is to open a way, remove obstructions, gain concentration, so that the Overself's grace can reach him. The union of both activities produces the result.

This identification with the best Self in us is the ideal set for all men, to be realized through long experience and much suffering or through accepting instruction, following revelation, unfolding intuition, practising meditation, and living wisely. . . .

Intellectual definitions of transcendental states merely leave us in the dark. We must practise walking on the divine path, and not merely talk about it, if we would know what these states really are.

This identification with the Overself is the real work set us, the real purpose for which human life in the world serves us. All else is merely a comfortable way of escape, a means of keeping us busy so that conscience need not be troubled by the central duty to which we are summoned.

Even while he travels on this quest he should habitually remind himself of an easily forgotten truth—that what he travels to is inside himself, is the very essence of himself.

What has never been lost can never be found. If a quester fails to find the Overself, it is not because of faults or weaknesses in the ego but because he is himself that which he seeks. There is nothing else to be found than understanding of this fact. . . .

Before the Overself can stay with you, the feelings must be brought to a condition of calm, the thoughts must be turned inwards and centered there. Otherwise the outer difficulties will not let go of your attention. . . .

Once he recognizes his responsibility toward the fulfilment of this higher purpose, for which the Infinite Wisdom has put him here, he will have to recognize also the obligation of devoting some time every day for study of, and meditation upon, it. . . .

From one point of view, the work done on the Quest is simply an uncovering of what is covered up: thoughts, emotions and passions, unceasing extroversion and never-ending egoism lie over the precious diamond like thick layers of earth. This is why the penetrative action of meditation is so necessary.

Constant reflection on metaphysical and ethical themes reaches a point where one day its accumulated weight pushes him around the corner into a mystical realization of those themes no less surely than meditation might have done.

Man as scientist has put under observation countless objects on earth, in sea and sky. He has thoroughly examined them. But man as man has put himself under a shallower observation. He has limited his scrutiny first to the body, second to what thinking can find. Yet a deeper level exists, where a deeper hidden self can be found.

The goals of progress are but imagined ones. There is only one goal which is undeniably real, completely certain, and authentically true—and that is an unchanging one, an eternal one. Yet it is also the one that has escaped mankind!

When we ask what is the purpose of the individual's existence, we shall find that the physical world can give us neither a complete nor a satisfying answer.

The businessman who does not know that the true business for which he was put on earth is to find the Overself, may make a fortune but will also squander away a lifetime. His work and mind have been left separate from his Overself's when they might have been kept in satisfying harmony with them.

Too much remembrance of the world leads to too much forgetfulness of the higher purpose of our life in the world.

❧

So long as thoughts remain unmastered, this present and personal experience shuts us out from reality.

❧

Our world is but a fleeting symbol, yet we may not disdain it. For it is the arched entrance under which we must pass through to the infinite life.

❧

When a man comes to the point when all his outer life dissolves in tragedy or calamity, he comes also to the point when this quest is all that is left to him. But he may not perceive this truth. He may miss his chance.

❧

There will always be opportunities for the follower of this path to put his philosophy into practice. Whether pleasant or unpleasant, they should be welcomed! The more he tries, the more he is likely to accomplish. He should take care not to depend upon his personal judgement alone. If he makes the beginnings of a right (that is, impersonal and egoless) response to each problem, help may mysteriously appear to guide him to a right solution. . . .

❧

Both desires and fears bind a man to his ego and thus bar the way to spiritual fulfilment. They could not exist except in relation to a second thing. But when he turns his mind away from all things and directs it toward its own still centre, it is the beginning of the end for all desires and all fears.

This Quest cannot be followed to success without the quality of courage. It is needed at the beginning, in the middle, and near the end. It is needed to think for oneself, to act in non-conformity to one's environment, and to obey intuitive leading toward new, unknown, or unfamiliar directions.

The iron strength of his purpose will shield him from temptations, the intense force of his loyalty to the truth will carry him through obstacles and barriers. He is astonished to find how easily the man who knows what he wants can conquer his way to it, if his will is able to go straight to its mark.

. . . he has first to establish the connection with the Overself so that its strength and understanding will then rule him effortlessly. The moment this connection is established, the aspirant will become aware of results from the descent of Divine Grace upon his personality. Such a moment is unpredictable, but, for the individual who sticks to the Quest, its arrival is sure.

He must look forward hopefully to the day when he can actually feel the higher self present within all his activity. It will reign in his inner world and thus be the real doer of his actions, not the ego in the outer world.

Slowly, as he strives onward with this inner work, his faults and frailties will fall away and this ever-shining better self hidden behind them will begin to be revealed.

If the teaching favourably commends itself to any individual from the first contact as being requisite to his needs, this is often a sign that he has followed it in earlier existences.

The time will come, if he perseveres, when his mind will naturally orient itself toward the spiritual pole of being. And this will happen by itself, without any urging on his part. No outer activity will be able to stop the process, for to make it possible his mind will apparently double its activity. In the foreground, it will attend to the outer world, but in the background it will attend to the Overself.

Anyone who pursued the Quest with the same zeal with which everyone pursues earthly things, would soon come within sight of its goal.

The effect of a full and proper absorption of these ideas is to strengthen a man and invigorate his purpose, to make him feel that what is behind the universe is behind him too.

The aspirant may have already discovered for himself some of the inner benefits of the Quest. Once the Overself has been experienced as a felt, living presence in the heart, it loosens the grip of egoistic desires—together with their emotional changes of mood—on one's consciousness and lifts it to a higher level, where he will soon become aware of a wonderful inner satisfaction which remains calm and unruffled despite outward circumstances to the contrary. . . .

Every test successfully met is rewarded by some growth in intuitive knowledge, strengthening of character, or initiation into a higher consciousness.

If philosophy begins with doubt and wonder, it ends by taking away whatever doubts are left in the mind and converting the wonder into holy reverence.

The Quest will come to an end when he turns away from teachers and teachings and begins to receive instruction from within himself. Previously all that he got was someone else's idea; now he is acquiring firsthand knowledge.

Before passing into a higher phase of his development, the disciple is usually confronted by life with a situation which will test his fitness for it. His success in meeting this test will open a gate leading to the next degree.

. . . The Overself waits with deepest patience for him—man—to prefer it completely to everything and everyone else. It waits for the time when longings for the soul will leave the true aspirant no rest, when love for the divine will outlast and outweigh all other loves. When he feels that he needs it more than he needs anything else in this world, the Overself will unfailingly reveal its presence to him. . . .

We fulfil life when we find ourselves in the divine presence unendingly, aware of it and expressing it.

The Short Path

The Quest has two aspects. One is the constant accumulation of right thoughts, feelings, and acts, along with the constant elimination of wrong ones. The other aspect called the Short Path is the constant remembrance and contemplation of the Overself.

Only at a well-advanced stage does the disciple begin to comprehend that his true work is not to develop qualities or achieve tasks, to evolve character or attain goals but to get rid of hindrances and pull aside veils. He has to desert the false self and uncover the true self.

The notion that the truth will be gained, that happiness will be achieved, that the Overself will be realized at the end of a long attempt must be seen as an illusory one. Truth, happiness, and the Overself must be seen in the Present, not the future, at the very beginning of his quest, not the end, here and now. . . .

Just as the ancient pagan Mysteries required some amount of preparation and some form of purification before candidates were admitted, so the Short Path ordinarily requires some Long Path work as a prerequisite. But not always and not now.

The essential features of the Long Path are its concern with moral effort and its emphasis on character building; its injunctions to pray and meditate; its insistence on the constant striving for self-mastery through physical, emotional, and mental disciplines. The essential feature of the Short Path is its quest of the flash of enlightenment through intuitive feeling and metaphysical thinking. Some believe, and would be satisfied with, this flash to be brief. Others hope for its permanent abidance.

. . . On the long path they are concerned with the personal ego and as a result give the negative thoughts their attention. On the short path they refuse to accept these negatives and instead look to the Overself. Thus the struggles will disappear. . . .

The Short Path is the real way! All else is mere preparation of the equipment for it. For with it he is no longer to direct his meditation upon the shortcomings and struggles of the personal self but up to the Overself, its presence and strength. For the consciousness of the Real, the True, the Beneficent and Peaceful comes by its Grace alone and by this practice he attracts the visitation.

Although it is quite correct to say that we grow through experience, that suffering has valuable lessons, and so on, we must also remember that these are only half-truths. The other half is that by Short Path identifications, we can so totally change our outlook that adverse experience becomes unnecessary.

. . . On the long path you must deal with the urges of interference arising from the lower self and the negativity which enters from the surrounding environment. But the efforts on the long path will at last invoke the grace, which opens the perspective of the short path. . . .

The Long Path calls for a continued effort of the will, the Short one for a continued loving attention.

The more he tries to fight the ego, the more he thinks about it and concentrates on it. This keeps him still its prisoner. Better is it to turn his back on it and think about, concentrate on the higher self.

He must not only do so far as he can all that the Long Path demands from him but he must also step outside it altogether and do those totally different things that the Short Path demands.

He can repudiate the man that he was in the past. . . . He can liberate himself from all the old images of himself and assume a new one, become a new man. For he can turn his back on all these ego-regarding attitudes and transfer his thoughts, his self-identification, to the Overself.

He learns that he may set his own limits, that so long as he thinks all day that he is only this person, doing and speaking in the ordinary way what men usually do, then he is certainly nothing more. But if he starts the day on a higher level, thinking that he is divine in his inmost being, and keeps on that level as the hours pass, then he will feel closer to it. This is a practical procedure, one which has its effect on consciousness, on character, and on events.

. . . After some measure of this preparation the aspirants enter the short path to complete this work. This takes a comparatively much shorter time and, as it has the possibility of yielding the full self-enlightenment at any moment, it ends suddenly. What they are trying to do on the long path continues by itself once they have entered fully on the short path. . . .

If, in his earlier days when on the Long Path, he practised daily checking his personal feelings where they were negative, hostile, or condemnatory in the relationship with others, or when they interrupted his inner calm in the relationship with himself, now on the Short Path he abandoned this training. It was no more the really important thing, for it had been just a preparation of the ego for that thing—which was to forget and transcend the ego by transferring attention to the remembrance of his divine being, his Overself.

The Long Path brings the self to a growing awareness of its own strength, whereas the Short Path brings it to a growing awareness of its own unreality. This higher stage leads inevitably to a turnaboutface, where the energies are directed toward identification with the One Infinite Mind. The more this is done, the more Grace flows by reaction into the Self.

The laborious, sometimes desperate self-discipline of the Long Path relaxes or even stops altogether. The effortless, sometimes ecstatic self-surrender to grace through faith, love, humility, and remembrance replaces it.

. . . The short path means that you begin to try to remember to live in the rarefied atmosphere of the Overself instead of worrying about the ego and measuring its spiritual development. . . .

Even those who are satisfied to continue permanently the Long Path's preparatory disciplines will one day find an inner impulse rising spontaneously within themselves and leading them to the Short Path.

Whatever path a man starts with, he must at the end of it come to the entrance of this path—the destruction of the illusion of the ego and giving up identification with it.

. . . He will not have to struggle as on the Long Path. There will no more be irksome effort. The mind will be glad to rest in this positive state, if he holds from the very beginning the faith that it already is accomplished, that the aspiration toward it is being fulfilled *now*, not at some unknown distant time. Such an attitude engenders something more than pleasant feelings of hope and optimism: it engenders subconscious power.

In the well-formed and well-informed aspirant the activities of both paths will be subtly blended. This is part of what is meant when it is said that he is properly balanced. And out of this union will come the "second birth," the new man who reflects at last the glorious consciousness of the Overself.

There is this difference when the Long Path is entered alone and when it is entered with the accompaniment of the Short one, that in the second case there is added the light of guidance, the protection of peace, the acceleration of progress, and the harmony of equilibrium.

While giving all attention to the Overself, or to its remembrance, or to its various aspects, or to the idea of it, he forgets himself. This makes it possible to transcend the ego. And this is why the Short Path *must* be travelled if the preparatory work of the other Path is to be completed.

The man on the Short Path moves forward directly to fulfil his objective. Instead of working by slow degrees toward the control of thoughts, he seeks to recollect the fact that the sacred Overself is present in his mind at this very moment, that It lives within him right now, and not only as a goal to be attained in some distant future. The more he understands this fact and holds attention to it, the more he finds himself able to feel the great calm which follows its realization, the more his thoughts automatically become still in consequence.

The Short Path calls for a definite change of mind, a thinking of totally new thoughts, a fastening of attention upon the goal instead of the way to it. It calls for a revolution, dethroning the ego from being the centre of attention and replacing it by the Overself.

This is the wonder of the Short Path—that it teaches us to refuse at once every thought which seeks to identify us with the feeble and unworthy self. This is the gladness of the Short Path—that it urges us to accept and hold only those thoughts which identify us directly with the strong and divine Overself, or which reflect its goodness and wisdom.

This is the concept which governs the Short Path: that he is in the Stillness of central being all the time whether he knows it or not, that he has never left and can never leave it. And this is so, even in a life passed in failure and despair.

. . . The basis of the Short Path is that we are always divine. It is with us already, it is no new thing, and we only have to try to recognize what is already there.

Here, on this Short Path, he is to direct his yearnings and seekings, his hopes and thoughts, solely to the Overself. Nothing and nobody, not even a guru, is to come between them.

What is the key to the Short Path? It is threefold. First, stop searching for the Overself since it follows you wherever you go. Second, believe in its Presence, with and within you. Third, keep on trying to understand its truth until you can abandon further thoughts about it. You cannot acquire what is already here. So drop the ego's false idea and affirm the real one.

The Short Path uses (a) *thinking*: metaphysical study of the Nature of Reality; (b) *practice*: constant remembrance of Reality during everyday life in the world; (c) *meditation*: surrender to the thought of Reality in stillness. You will observe that in all these three activities *there is no reference to the personal ego.* There is no thinking of, remembering, or meditating upon oneself, as there is with the Long Path.

A part of the Short Path work is intellectual study of the metaphysics of Truth. This is needful to expose the ego's own illusoriness, as a preliminary to transcending it, and to discriminate its ideas, however spiritual, from reality.

For if we are divine and timeless beings now (and who can gainsay it that has had a glimpse of that starry state memorably vouchsafed to him?) then we have always been such. How can we evolve who are already self-existent, perfect beings? Does it not seem more probable that something alien has accreted around us, covering up the sublimer consciousness; that Time's work is not to raise us but to free us; that our search is not for a loftier state but for our *pristine* state, to recover our former grandeur? What we need is not to grow but to know. Evolution cannot help us, but *self*-knowledge can.

On the Short Path he fixes his mind on divine attributes, such as the all-pervading, ever-present, beginningless and endless nature of the One Life-Power, until he is lifted out of his little ego entirely.

. . . the Short Path . . . makes life considerably pleasanter because you are supposed to make a 180 degree turn, putting your past behind you, looking first on the bright side, the sunny side, of your spiritual life. Very often a glimpse is given which starts you off on the Short Path. . . .

He cultivates a more joyous attitude, this man on the Short Path, for remembrance of the Overself, which he practises constantly, reminds him of the glory of the Overself.

The Short Path provides him with the chance of making a fresh start, of gaining new inspiration, more joy.

When he can release himself from the ego's tyranny and relate himself to the Overself's guidance, an entirely new life will open up for him.

As his centre moves to a profounder depth of being, peace of mind becomes increasingly a constant companion. This in turn influences the way in which he handles his share of the world's activities. Impatience and stupidity recede, wrath at malignity is disciplined; discouragement under adversity is controlled and stress under pressures relaxed.

It is a Short Path attitude to avoid censorious reproaches and condemnatory speech—these as a part of its larger rejection of negatives and preference for positives.

Reject every negative thought with implacable rigour—this is one of the important practical deductions of the Short Path.

. . . In moments of exaltation, uplift, awe, or satisfaction—derived from music, art, poetry, landscape, or otherwise—thousands of people have received a Glimpse; but only those on the Short Path recognize it for what it really is.

Think of yourself as the individual and you are sure to die; think of yourself as the universal and you enter deathlessness, for the universal is always and eternally there. We know no beginning and no ending to the cosmic process. Its being IS: we can say no more. Be that rather than this—that which is as infinite and homeless as space, that which is timeless and unbroken. Take the whole of life as your own being. Do not divorce, do not separate yourself from it. It is the hardest of tasks for it demands that we see our own relative insignificance amid this infinite and vast process. The change that is needed is entirely a mental one. Change your outlook and with it "heaven will be added unto you."

The real Short Path is really the discovery that there is no path at all: only a being still and thus letting the Overself do the work needed. This is the meaning of grace.

There is really nothing to be achieved here; only something to be accepted—the fact of your own divinity.

To make progress inwardly is ultimately all that matters, everything else passes except the fruit of our spiritual efforts.

. . . To summarize the entire process, the Long Path leads to the Short Path, and the Short Path leads to the Grace of an unbroken egoless consciousness.

Always Remember

The Short Path is, in essence, the ceaseless practice of remembering to stay in the Stillness, for this is what he really is in his innermost being and where he meets the World-Mind.

Continuous remembrance of the Stillness, accompanied by automatic entry into it, is the sum and substance of the Short Path, the key practice to success. At all times, under all circumstances, this is to be done. That is to say, it really belongs to and is part of the daily and ordinary routine existence. Consequently, whenever it is forgotten, the practitioner must note his failure and make instant correction. The inner work is kept up until it goes on by itself.

The best way to honour this immense truth of the ever-present reality of the Overself is to *remember* it—as often, as continuously, and as determinedly as possible. It is not only the best way but also the most rewarding one. For then its saving grace may bestow great blessing.

. . . The "remembrance exercise" consists of trying to recall the glimpse of the Overself, not only during the set meditation periods but also in each moment during the whole working span of the day—in the same way as a mother who has lost her child can not let go of the thought of it no matter what she is doing outwardly, or as a lover who constantly holds the vivid image of the beloved in the back of his mind. In a similar way, you keep the memory of the Overself alive during this exercise and let it shine in the background while you go about your daily work. But the spirit of the exercise is not to be lost. It must not be mechanical and cold. The time may come later when the remembrance will cease as a consciously and deliberately willed exercise and pass by itself into a state which will be maintained without the help of the ego's will. . . .

He learns to look away from the ego and turn to the Overself. He keeps his thoughts as often as possible on the remembrance of the latter's infinite ever-presence. He keeps his heart occupied with the feelings of peace, faith, harmony, and freedom that this remembrance generates.

The method of this exercise is to maintain uninterruptedly and unbrokenly the remembrance of the soul's nearness, the soul's reality, the soul's transcendence. The goal of this exercise is to become wholly possessed by the soul itself.

He must think as often and as intently of the Overself as an infatuated girl thinks of the next appointed meeting with her lover. His whole heart must be held captive, as it were, by this aspiration. This is to be practised not only at set formal times but also constantly throughout the day as an exercise in recollection. This yoga, done at all times and in all places, becomes a permanent life and not merely a transient exercise. This practice of constant remembrance of the Overself purifies the mind and gradually renders it naturally introverted, concentrates and eventually illumines it.

There is no moment when this work of inner remembrance may stop. It ought to start at the time of rising from bed in the morning and continue to the time of retiring to bed at night.

You should imaginatively recapture it as if its benign presence comes over you, its goodwill pervades you, its guidance helps you, and its peace enfolds you.

He will come to perceive that his real strength lies in remembering the higher self, in remembering the quest of it, and, above all, in remembering the two with intense love, devotion, and faith.

How long should a man practise this remembrance of the Overself? He will need to practise it so long as he needs to struggle with his ego.

This notion that we must wait and wait while we slowly progress out of enslavement into liberation, out of ignorance into knowledge, out of the present limitations into a future union with the Divine, is only true if we let it be so. But we need not. We can shift our identification from the ego to the Overself in our habitual thinking, in our daily reactions and attitudes, in our response to events and the world. We have thought our way into this unsatisfactory state; we can unthink our way out of it. By incessantly remembering what we really are, here and now at this very moment, we set ourselves free. Why wait for what already is?

❦

By thought, the ego was made; by thought, the ego's power can be unmade. But the thought must be directed toward a higher entity, for the ego's willingness to attack itself is only a pretense. Direct it constantly to the Overself, be mentally devoted to the Overself, and emotionally love the Overself. Can it then refuse to help you?

❦

Whatever you do to work upon the ego, whether you remove this weakness or improve that faculty, it will always be ego and your consciousness will always remain within its tightly closed circle. In the time you give to such work you could be occupying yourself with thought of the non-ego, the Overself, and dwelling in this thought until the sunshine behind it bursts through and you bask in the glory.

❦

The appearance of the sacred presence automatically extinguishes the lower desires. The holding on to that presence wherever he goes and whatever he does as if it were his real identity, will help to establish that release as a lasting fact.

❦

. . . In times of actual danger, the calm remembrance of the Overself will help to protect him.

❦

He has gone far on this path when his last thought on falling asleep at night is the Overself and his first thought on waking up in the morning is again the Overself.

This constant remembrance of the higher self becomes in time like a kind of holy communion.

To forget self but to remember Overself—it is as simple as that, and also as hard as that.

As If . . .

. . . The remembrance is a necessary preparation for the second exercise, in which you try to obtain an immediate identification with the Overself. Just as an actor identifies with the role he plays on the stage, you act *think* and live during the daily life "as if" *you* were the Overself. This exercise is not merely intellectual but also includes feeling and intuitive action. It is an act of creative imagination in which by turning directly to playing the part of the Overself you make it possible for its grace to come more and more into your life.

A part of the practical technique for attaining the inner awareness of this timeless reality is the practice of the AS IF exercise. . . . The practitioner regards himself no longer from the standpoint of the quester, but from that of the Realized Man. He assumes, in thought and action, that he has nothing to attain. . . .

. . . He is to see himself doing successfully what he seeks to do, and the sight is to be accompanied by intense faith and firm conviction. The desirable qualities of character are to be thought of as already existing and possessed, already expressing themselves in action and living. Furthermore they are to be pictured vividly and clearly; they must be understood without any uncertainty, dimness, or hesitation.

Let him picture his own self as if it were at the end of its quest. Let him see it enthroned on the summit of power and engaged in tranquil meditation for his own joy and for mankind's welfare.

. . . he accepts the truth, passed down to him by the Enlightened Ones, that in his inmost essence he is Reality. This leads to the logical consequence that he should disregard personal feelings which continue from past tendencies, habits, attitudes, and think and act as if he were himself an enlightened one! . . .

. . . through the understanding of the Short Path he searches knowingly, not wanting another experience since both wanting and experiencing put him out of the essential Self. He thinks and acts as if he is that Self, which puts him back into It. . . .

Practice of the "As If" exercise is like being spiritually reborn and finding a new way of life. It gives courage to those who feel grievously inadequate, hope to those who feel hooked by their past failures.

This practice of picturing oneself as one ought to be, of visualizing the man free from negative qualities and radiant with positive ones that are part of the Quest's ideal, has near-magical results.

Even if he has no spiritual experience at all but only complete faith in it, even if he cannot live the role of the illumined fulfilled man, then let him act it. This is an exercise to be practised. Let him try to think and behave as if his quest is successful, let him copy the fulfilled philosopher.

Mental Quiet

There are different kinds of meditation. The elementary is concerned with holding certain thoughts firmly in the mind. The advanced is concerned with keeping all thoughts completely out of the mind. The highest is concerned with merging the mind blissfully in the Overself.

A day begun with mental quiet and inner receptivity is a day whose work is well begun. Every idea, decision, move, or action which flows out from it later will be wiser better and nobler than it otherwise would have been.

. . . Meditation should be opened by silent prayer, formulated to express spiritual yearnings for the higher way of life. This may be followed by concentrating on a chosen spiritual theme. Every endeavour should be made to keep thoughts from wandering and to bring them back whenever they do.

Both prayer and receptivity are needed. First we pray fervently and feelingly to the Overself to draw us closer to it, then we lapse into emotional quietness and patiently wait to let the inner self unfold to us. There is no need to discard prayer because we take up meditation. The one makes a fit prelude to the other. The real need is to purify prayer and uplift its objectives.

The attempt to get rid of the faults and evils in oneself by using the powers of concentration and meditation belongs to the Long Path. But it is still occupied with the ego. For those who have turned to the Short Path, the object of meditation is entirely changed. It is no longer occupied with purifying, improving, or bettering the ego—it is occupied only with the transcendent self, and the thought of the ego, the remembrance of it, is left behind altogether.

This is one of the subtlest acts which anyone can perform, this becoming conscious of consciousness, this attending to attention.

. . . The pure philosophic meditation as ultimately sought and reached on the Short Path is to put the attention directly on the Overself and on nothing else.

There is a single basic principle which runs like a thread through all these higher contemplation exercises. It is this: if we can desert the thoughts of particular things, the images of particular objects raised by the senses in the field of consciousness, and if we can do this with complete and intelligent understanding of what we are doing and why we are doing it, then such desertion will be followed by the appearance of its own accord of the element of pure undifferentiated Thought itself; the latter will be identified as our innermost self.

Because thinking is an activity within time, it cannot lead to the Timeless. For this attainment, mental quiet is necessary.

He will understand the real spirit of meditation when he understands that he has to do nothing at all, just to sit still physically, mentally, and emotionally. For the moment he attempts to do anything, he intrudes his ego. By sitting inwardly and outwardly still, he surrenders egoistic action and thereby implies that he is willing to surrender his little self to his Overself. He shows that he is willing to step aside and let himself be worked upon, acted through, and guided by a higher power.

. . . If he has ever had a glimpse of a supersensuous higher existence which profoundly impressed him and perhaps led him to take to the quest, it is *most important* that he should also insert the remembrance of this experience into his exercise. He

should try to bring as vividly as possible to his mind the sense
of peace and exaltation which he then felt. . . .

⁊

It is not just ceasing to think, although it prerequires that, but
something more: it is also a positive alertness to the Divine
Presence.

⁊

The Overself is drawing him ever inward to Itself, but the
ego's earthly nature is drawing him back to all those things or
activities which keep him outwardly busy. On the issue of this
tension depends the result of his meditation. If he can bring
such devotion to the Overself that out of it he can find enough
strength to put aside everything else that he may be doing or
thinking and give himself up for a while to dwelling solely
in it, this is the same as denying himself and his activities.
Once his little self gets out of the way, success in reaching the
Overself is near.

⁊

As the mind's movement ebbs away and its turnings slow down,
the ego's desires for, and attempt to hold on to, its world drop
away. What ensues is a real mental quiet. The man discovers
himself, his Overself.

⁊

When the student attains to this stage of meditation, all sen-
sations of an external world sink away but the idea of his own
abstract existence still remains. His next effort must therefore
be to suppress this idea and if he succeeds then this is followed
by a sense of infinity.

Thinking can, ordinarily, only produce more thoughts. Even thinking about truth, about reality, however correct it be, shares this limitation. But if properly instructed it will know its place and understand the situation, with the consequence that at the proper moment it will make no further effort, and will seek to merge into meditation. When the merger is successfully completed, a holy silence will pervade the consciousness which remains. Truth will then be revealed of its own accord.

The attention must be concentrated at this stage solely on the hidden soul. No other aim and even no symbol of It may now be held. When he has become so profoundly absorbed in this contemplation that his whole being, his whole psyche of thought, feeling, will, and intuition are mingled and blent in it, there may come suddenly and unexpectedly a displacement of awareness. He actually *passes out* of what he has hitherto known as himself into a new dimension and becomes a different being. . . .

When consciousness is stripped of its contents and stands in naked simplicity so that it can be seen as it really is, a tremendous quietude falls upon us. All strivings cease of their own accord.

❧

There are moments when the Overself gets at a man's consciousness, and rarer moments when he gets at Its consciousness. It is his profit to extend them, if he can, or to dwell long and often on their memory, if he cannot. . . . Whenever he notices the very slightest indrawing to the Overself, whenever the least feeling of Its onset appears, he should *at once* begin to wrap himself around with the felt influence to the exclusion of everything else.

The faculty of attention is interiorized and turned back upon itself.

As he sinks deeper after many relapses towards the undivided mind, as he calls on all the powers of his will and concentration to keep within focus the inner work of this spiritual exercise, he may get a sense of leading, of being directed by something within.

Follow this invisible thread of tender holy feeling, keep attention close to it, do not let other things distract or bring you away from it. For at its end is entry into Awareness.

To achieve this kind of concentration where attention is withdrawn from the outer world and held tightly in itself, a determined attitude is needed of not stopping until this sharply pointed state is reached. All other thoughts are rejected in the very moment that they arise. If at the start there is aspiration and devotion toward the Overself, and in the course of the effort too, then eventually the stress falls away and the Stillness replaces it.

Withdrawn from the world's clamour to this still centre of his innermost being, waiting in utter patience for the Presence which may or may not appear, he performs a daily duty which has become of high importance and priority.

When this turning inwards completes itself in the final state of contemplation so that thought is stilled and breath is quiet, the sense of succession is dispelled, a kind of continuous now takes its place, and a stillness of the body corresponds with a stillness of the mind.

Contemplation is attained when your thinking about a spiritual truth or about the spiritual goal suddenly ceases of itself. The mind then enters into a perfectly still and rapt condition.

Memorable are those minutes when we sit in silent adoration of the Overself, knowing it to be none other than our own best self. It is as though we have returned to our true home and rest by its hallowed hearth with a contentment nowhere else to be known. No longer do we possess anything; we are ourselves ineffably possessed. . . .

. . . When the personal mind is stripped of its memories and anticipations, when all sense-impressions and thoughts entirely drop away from it, then it enters the realm of empty unnameable Nothingness. It is really a kind of self-contemplation. But this self is not finite and individual, it is cosmic and infinite.

The threshold of this inner being cannot be crossed without overcoming the fear that arises on reaching it. This is a fear of the unknown, the unfamiliar, the fantastic, and the illusory. The ego shrinks back from what is so strange to its past experience. It is afraid of losing itself in this emptiness that confronts it, and with that losing hold of the solid ground of physical life. Only by calling up all its inner courage and inner strength can these enemies be conquered.

Paradoxically enough, tremendous forces lie latent here. Indeed the law is that the deeper a man penetrates into the void and the longer he sustains this penetration, the greater will be the power with which he will emerge from it.

He feels that he is now in the very centre of his being, that he has shifted identity there. The ego no longer covers it over and occupies his whole view. Rather is it now transparent to the light radiating from this centre. This transparency is peace.

There is no need to yield to the fear of the void, which comes in the deepest meditation. That is merely the personal ego offering its resistance to the higher self. That same fear of never being able to come back has to be faced by all advanced mystics when they reach this stage of meditation, but it is utterly groundless and is really a test of faith in God to protect them in a most laudable endeavour: to come closer to him and to advance farther from their lower self. . . .

Just then, as thoughts themselves stop coming into his mind, he stops living in time and begins living in the eternal. He knows and feels his timelessness. And since all his sufferings belong to the world of passing time, of personal ego, he leaves them far behind as though they had never been. He finds himself in the heaven of a serene, infinite bliss. He learns that he could always have entered it; only his insistence on holding to the little egoistic values, his lack of thought-control, and his disobedience to the age-old advice of the Great Teachers prevented him from doing so.

We enter into paradise when, in contemplation, we enter into awareness of the Overself.

This stillness is the godlike part of every human being. In failing to look for it, he fails to make the most of his possibilities. If, looking, he misses it on the way, this happens because it is a vacuity: there is simply nothing there! That means no things, not even mental things, that is, thoughts.

The higher purpose of meditation is missed if it does not end in the peace, the stillness, that emanates from the real self. However slightly it may be felt, this is the essential work which meditation must do for us.

. . . Overself is only an *object* of meditation so long as he knows it only as something apart from himself. That is good but not good enough. For he is worshipping a graven image, not the sublime reality. He has to rise still higher and reach it, not as a separate "other," but as his very self.

Both the necessity and justification of meditation lie in this, that man is so preoccupied with his own thoughts that he is never aware of the mind out of which they arise and in which they vanish. The process of stilling these thoughts, or advanced meditation, makes this awareness possible.

The exercise of watching a thought arise and vanish and then intently holding on to the interval before the next thought arises, is a hard one. It needs months and years of patient practice. But the reward, when it comes, is immense.

No system of education can be a complete or an adequate one if it omits to teach young persons how to meditate. This is the one art which can assist them not only to develop self-control and to improve character but also to master all the other arts through mastery of concentration. . . .

The portrayal of Gautama as a seated meditating figure symbolizes his basic message. This was really, and quite simply, "Be still—empty yourself—let out the thoughts, the desires, and the ego which prevent this inner stillness."

. . . It is no truer message than this: "Seek for the divine within yourself, return to it every day, learn how to continue in it and finally *be* it."

The practice of extending love towards all living creatures brings on ecstatic states of cosmic joy.

The Witness

. . . Here, then, is the first practice of the ultimate path: think constantly of that Mind which is producing the ego, all the other egos around, and all the world, in fact. Keep this up until it becomes habitual. The consequence is that one tends in time to regard his own ego with complete detachment, as though he were regarding somebody else. Furthermore, it forces him to take the standpoint of the *all*, and to see unity as fundamental being. . . .

The quest is a deliberate attempt to shorten the passage from life in the underself to life in the Overself. Therefore it involves a constant discipline of actions, feelings, thoughts, and words.

Even while you share in the life, the work, and the pleasures of this world, learn also to stand aside as a witness of them all. Learn how to be a spectator as well as a participator; in short, let detachment accompany your involvement, or rather let it hide secretly behind the other. . . .

He will have to learn the art of standing aside from himself, of observing his actions and analysing his motives as though they belonged to some other person. He may cease to practise this art only when his actions reflect the calm wisdom of the Overself and when his motives reflect its detached impersonality.

~

Let him play the part of a witness to his own ego, through all its experiences and vicissitudes. In that way he will be emulating by effort those enlightened men to whom the part comes easily and naturally by their own development.

~

To play the role of an observer of life, his own life, is to assist the process of inwardly detaching himself from it. And the field of observation must include the mental events, the thought-happenings, also. . . .

~

The student has to stand aside from the thought-forms, which means that he must stand aside from the person and look at it as something external to himself. If and when he succeeds in getting behind it, he automatically adopts the standpoint of the Overself. He must make the person an object and the Overself its observer. . . .

~

Every time he departs from the stillness there is needed a warning awareness. This does not easily or normally come by itself but by self-training, self-observation— "mindfulness," the Buddha called it. . . .

To practise living in the world and yet not being of it involves becoming a spectator not only of the world but also of oneself. To the extent that he gets lost in the world-experience, to that extent he loses this deeper self-awareness.

By adopting a witness attitude he puts a distance between the day's activities and himself. This helps him bring them under control, prevents them from submerging his quest altogether, and preserves whatever inner peace he attains.

When he can mentally withdraw at will from a situation where he is involved with others, so as to regard all the parties, including himself, with calm impartiality, he will have travelled far.

He may come in time to feel a certain amusement at watching his own performance on the stage of life.

Aspiration for a Higher Life

A double work goes on: the man slowly withdraws from the things which hold him, which make him theirs, while his higher aspirations attract the higher self to slowly take over the place in his heart which they filled.

It is the presence of the Overself in us that creates the germ of our aspirations for a higher life. It is the warm sunshine and cold rain of experience that nurtures the germ. It is the influence of spiritual individuals that brings the growth through its varying stages.

This moving of consciousness to a higher level will come about by itself, if the calm is patiently allowed to settle itself down sufficiently, and if there has been preparation by study, aspiration, and purification.

Whoever seeks this intimate awareness of the Overself-presence does not need to seek anywhere outside his own heart and mind, does not really need to go to any distant land nor try to find some other person to become his "Master." . . .

At intervals, on certain grave, joyous, or relaxed occasions, he may feel a deep nostalgia for what he may only dimly and vaguely comprehend. He may name it, in ignorance, otherwise but it will really be for his true spiritual source.

When a man passes from the self-seeking motives of the multitude to the Overself-seeking aspirations of the Quest, he passes to conscious co-operation with the Divine World-Idea.

. . . without the yearning the advent of Grace is unlikely, and without Grace there can never be any realization of the Overself. . . .

⤋

The desire to get at the soul must become so predominant and so anxious that a continuous tension is created within him.

⤋

The spiritual awakening can come to mankind only as it comes to individuals—after it is strongly desired by the individual himself; and it will be desired only when all other desires have been tried and found wanting.

⤋

. . . When he feels the urge to weep for no apparent reason he should not resist, as it is a sign of the working of Grace upon him. The more he yields to this urge the more quickly will he progress. This is an important manifestation although its inner significance will not be understood by the materialistic world.

⤋

The timetable of a seeker's advance depends on several factors, but without doubt the most important of them all is the strength of the longing within his heart for the Highest.

⤋

We are like flowers torn from our natural soil and suffering the misery of separation. Our fervid mystical yearnings represent the recognition of our need to reunite with our Source.

Loving Surrender

He has access to infinite wisdom and infinite support in every situation and under every given circumstance. But he has it only so far as he submits the ego to the higher self.

When it seems humanly impossible to do more in a difficult situation, surrender yourself to the inner silence and thereafter wait for a sign of obvious guidance or for a renewal of inner strength.

The passage from black despair to healing peace begins with learning to "let go." This can refer to the past's crippling pictures, the present's harsh conditions, or the future's grim anticipations. To what then can the sufferer turn? To the Overself and its divine power.

Take your peril to the Overself, identify your real being with the Overself and not with the vanishing ego. Then you will be at the standpoint which perceives that you are as secure and safe as the Overself is. Hold your position as the final and highest one. Reject the very thought of being in danger. There is none in the Overself.

The surrender of every problem as it arises to the higher self, the renouncing of personal will in the matter, and the readiness to accept intuitive guidance as and when it comes provide a superior technique and yield better results than the old ways of intellectual handling and personal planning alone.

What it is necessary for him to do is really to surrender his fears and anxieties, whether concerning himself or those near and dear to him, or those who, he thinks, want to hurt him. He should surrender all these to God and be himself rid of them. For this is what giving up the ego truly means. He would then have no need to entertain such negative thoughts. They would be replaced by a strong faith that all would be well with him. To the extent that he can give up the little ego with its desires and fears, to that extent he invites and attracts divine help in his life.

. . . Every time he patiently crushes a wrong or foolish thought, he adds to his inner strength. Every time he bravely faces up to a misfortune with calm impersonal appraisal of its lesson, he adds to his inner wisdom. The man who has thus wisely and self-critically surrendered himself may then go forward with a sense of outward security and inward assurance, hopeful and unafraid, because he is now aware of the benign protection of his Overself. . . .

You will have turned over the matter or problem if certain signs appear: first, no more anxiety or fretting about it; second, no more stress or tension over it; third, no more deliberating and thinking concerning it.

The surrender to the Overself must not be misinterpreted as surrender to lethargy, to lack of initiative, or to absence of effort. It means that before initiative rises and before effort is made, a man will first look to the Overself for inspiration. When such inner guidance and rational thinking speak with united voice, then he can go forward with a plan, a faith, or a deed, sure and unafraid and confident.

※

If he turns his problem over to the Overself in unreserved trust, he must admit no thoughts thereafter of doubt or fear. If they still knock at his door he must respond by remembering his surrender.

※

Although the price of attainment, which is the gradual giving up of the lower self, is agonizing because the lower one is the only self we know ordinarily, there is for every such surrender a compensation equal in value at least to what is given up, and actually of more surpassing worth. This compensation is not only a theoretical one, it is a real experience; and at the last, when the whole of the lesser self is surrendered, the only description of it which mere words can give is blissful peace. Since agony of mind cannot coexist with peace, the agony falls away and only the peace remains. The warning must be given, however, that the Higher Self never yields its compensations until the requisite surrender is made. If this is done little by little, which is usually the only way it can be done, then the lovely compensation will follow also little by little.

※

. . . At a certain stage he must learn to "let go" more and allow the Overself to possess him, rather than strain to possess something which he believes to be still eluding him. Every aspirant who has passed it will remember how he leapt ahead when he made this discovery. . . .

The indispensable prerequisite to mystical illumination is self-surrender. No man can receive it without paying this price. . . .

"How am I to start upon this process of true self-knowledge?" The answer begins with this: first adopt the right attitude. *Believe* in the divinity of your deeper self. Stop looking elsewhere for light, stop wandering hither and thither for power. . . . engrave on your heart the high phrases: "I possess illimitable power *within* me; I *can* create a diviner life and truer vision than I now possess." Do this and then surrender your body, your heart and mind to the Infinite Power which sustains all. Strive to obey Its inward promptings and then declare your readiness to accept whatsoever lot it assigns you. This is your challenge to the gods and they will surely answer you. Your soul will be slowly or suddenly liberated; your body will be granted a freer pathway through conditions. . . .

. . . The Quest of the divine soul has become his pole star. It was natural for him to feel repelled at first by the idea of over-coming the ego but now he sees its desirability. This will not mean giving it up in practical life however; for while he is in the flesh the ideal is to find a proper balance between egoism and altruism because he needs both. . . .

It is the poor ego which worries and struggles to come closer to perfection. But how can the imperfect ever transform itself into the perfect? Let it cease its worry and simply surrender itself to the ever-perfect Overself.

No one else can do for a man what Nature is tutoring him to do for himself, that is, to surrender the ego to the higher self. Without such surrender no man can attain the consciousness of that higher self. It is useless to look to a master to make for him this tremendous change-over within himself. No master could do it. The proper way and the only way is to give up this pathetic clinging to his own power, to his own littleness, and to his own limitations. . . .

When a man consciously asks for union with the Overself, he unconsciously accepts the condition that goes along with it, and that is to give himself wholly up to the Overself. . . .

Such is the strange paradox of the quest that on the one hand he must foster determined self-reliance but on the other yield to a feeling of utter dependence on the higher powers.

We achieve a total surrender of the ego only when we cease to identify ourselves with it. In this aspiration is the key to a practical method of achievement.

So long as he is more afraid of giving up the ego than he is desirous of gaining the consciousness beyond it, so long will he dwell in its gloom.

To all things there is an equivalent price. For awareness of the Overself, pay with the thing that blocks your way—sacrifice the ego.

If he wants the full Grace he must make the full surrender. He should ask for nothing else than to be taken up wholly into, and by, the Overself. To ask for occult powers of any kind, even the kind which are called spiritual healing powers, is to ask for something less than this.

His destination is also his origin. But to say that he was born in the eternal Spirit starts the question, "How can time, which is placed outside eternity, bring him to eternity?" The answer is that it does not bring him there; it only educates him to look for, and prepares him to pass through, the opening through which he can escape. Need it be said that this lies at the point where ego surrenders wholly to Overself?

The more he gives himself up to the Overself as a consequence of these glimpses of what it requires of him, the sooner will their transience be transformed into permanence.

He knows, having aligned himself harmoniously with the higher power that supports the universe, that it surely can and will support the little fragment of the universe that is himself. A sublime confidence that he will be taken care of in the proper way pervades him in consequence.

. . . A day will break surely when every man will have to bend the knee to that unknown self and abandon every cell of his brain, every flowing molecule of his heart, his blood, into its waiting hands. Though he will fear to do so, though he will fear to give up those ancient idols who had held him in bond so long and have given him so little in return, though he will tremble to loose his moorings and let his soul drift slowly from them with sails set for that mysterious region whose longitude few men know and whose shores most men shun, yet he will do so all the same. . . .

If men only knew how glorious, how rich, how satisfying this inner life really is, they would not hesitate for a moment to forsake all those things which bar their way to it.

7

The Wonder of Grace

. . . The very fact that a man has consciously begun the quest is itself a manifestation of Grace, for he has begun to seek the Overself only because the Overself's own working has begun to make it plain to him, through the sense of unbearable separation from it, that the right moment for this has arrived. The aspirant should therefore take heart and feel hope. He is not really walking alone. The very love which has awakened within him for the Overself is a reflection of the love which is being shown towards him. . . .

. . . Man's initiative pushes on toward the goal, whilst divine Grace draws him to it. Both forces must combine if the process is to be completed and crowned with success. Yet that which originally made the goal attractive to him and inspired him with faith in it and thus gave rise to his efforts, was itself the Grace. . . .

Grace is a cosmic fact. If it were not, then the spiritual outlook for the human race, dependent entirely on its own efforts for the possibility of spiritual progress, would be poor and disheartening.

Grace Takes Us . . .

There is a power which inspires the heart, enlightens the mind, and sanctifies the character of man. It is the power of Grace.

The ineffable peace and exquisite harmony which take hold of his heart are the first results of grace.

Grace is of two kinds. The ordinary, better known, and inferior kind is that which is found on the Long Path. It flows from the Overself in automatic response to intense faith or devotion, expressed during a time of need. It is a reaction to seeking for help. The rarer and superior kind is found on the Short Path. It arises from self-identification with the Overself or constant recollection of it. There is no ego here to seek help or to call for a Grace which is necessarily ever present in the Overself.

The destiny of the ego is to be lifted up into the Overself, and there end itself or, more correctly, transcend itself. But because it will not willingly bring its own life to a cessation, some power from outside must intervene to effect the lifting up. That power is Grace and this is the reason why the appearance of Grace is imperative. . . .

. . . Thus the very search upon which he has embarked, the studies he is making, and the meditations he is practising are all inspired by the Overself from the beginning and sustained by it to the end. The Overself is already at work even before he begins to seek it. Indeed he has taken to the quest in unconscious obedience to the divine prompting. And that prompting is the first movement of Grace. Even when he believes that he is doing these things for himself, it is really Grace that is opening the heart and enlightening the mind from behind the scenes. . . .

What Grace does is to draw the man's attention away from himself, from his ego, to the Overself.

It is an inner emptiness gained by casting out desires and attachments, habits and tendencies, so that the heart is wide open to receive life's greatest gift—Grace. The craving to acquire personal possessions is a hard thing to still but once done we are rewarded a hundredfold.

He may know that the work of Grace has begun when he feels an active drawing from within which wakes him from sleep and which recurs in the day, urging him to practise his devotions, his recollections, his prayers, or his meditations. It leads him from his surface consciousness to his inner being, a movement which slowly goes back in ever-deepening exploration and discovery of himself.

⁓

If there is any law connected with grace, it is that as we give love to the Overself so do we get grace from it. . . .

⁓

The closer he comes to the Overself, the more actively is the Grace able to operate on him. The reason for this lies in the very nature of Grace, since it is nothing other than a benign force emanating from the Overself. It is always there but is prevented by the dominance of the animal nature and the ego from entering his awareness. When this dominance is sufficiently broken down, the Grace comes into play more and more frequently, both through Glimpses and otherwise.

⁓

The real bar to the entry of grace is simply the preoccupation of his thoughts with himself. For then the Overself must leave him to his cares.

⁓

When the Grace has led him sufficiently far, he will be distinctly aware of an inner presence. It will think for him, feel for him, and even act for him. This is the beginning of, and what it means to have, an egoless life.

⁓

. . . When the remembrance becomes ceaseless flow, the Overself will bring him a remarkable fruitage of grace. When he turns habitually inwards toward the Overself, grace can operate more readily in all matters. When the grace starts working, this is likely to remove a number of internal and external obstacles in his path—sometimes in a seemingly miraculous manner—and eventually bring him to a truer self-awareness.

It is not by special intervention that the divine grace appears in his life. For it was there all the time, and behind all his struggles, as a constant unbroken radiation from the Overself. But those struggles were like the hoisting of sails on a ship. Once up, they are able to catch the wind and propulsion begins automatically.

Why should the Short Path be a better means of getting Grace than the Long one? There is not only the reason that it is not occupied with the ego but also that it continually keeps up remembrance of the Overself. It does this with a heart that gives, and is open to receive, love. It thinks of the Overself throughout the day. Thus, it not only comes closer to the source from which Grace is being perpetually radiated, but it also is repeatedly inviting Grace with each loving remembrance.

To keep the Overself constantly in our thoughts is one of the easiest ways to become worthy of its grace.

Do not think so much of looking for outside help. Your Higher Self is with you. If you could have enough faith in its presence, you could look inwards. With persistence and patience, it would guide you.

Grace is here for all. It cannot be here for one special person and not for another. Only we do not know how to open our tensioned hands and receive it, how to open our ego-tight hearts and let it gently enter.

. . . In the moment that a man willingly deserts his habitual standpoint under a trying situation and substitutes this higher one, in that moment he receives Grace. With this reception a miracle is performed and the evil of the lower standpoint is permanently expelled from his character. The situation itself both put him to the proof and gave him his chance. . . .

. . . The mysterious intrusion of Grace may change the course of events. It introduces new possibilities, a different current of destiny. . . .

By this grace the past's errors may be forgotten so that the present's healing may be accepted. In the joy of this grace, the misery of old mistakes may be banished forever. Do not return to the past—live only in the eternal Now—in its peace, love, wisdom, and strength.

Many have failed to disidentify themselves from their thoughts, despite all attempts. This shows its difficulty, not its impossibility. In such cases, grace alone will liberate them from their thought-chains.

In the early stages of spiritual progress, Grace may show itself in the bestowal of ecstatic emotions. This encourages him to pursue the Quest and to know that he is so far pursuing it rightly. But the purpose gained, the blissful states will eventually pass away, as they must. He will then falsely imagine that he has lost Grace, that he has left undone something he should have done or done something he should not have done. The true fact is that it is Grace itself which has brought this loss about, as constituting his next stage of progress. . . .

If with the purpose of seeking to disidentify himself with the ego a man practises the necessary self-denial, makes the requisite sacrifices, and trains his thoughts and feelings, after a certain time and at a certain point of his path the forces of heaven will come to him to complete the work which he has started.

. . . When his own personal effort subsides, a further effort begins on his behalf by a higher power. Without any move on his own part, Grace begins to do for him what he could not do for himself, and under its beneficent operation he will find his higher will strengthening, his moral attitude improving, and his spiritual aspiration increasing. . . .

. . . into the Shining Presence

In that last battle when he comes face to face with the ego, when it has to put off all its protective disguises and expose its vulnerability, he must call upon the help of Grace. He cannot possibly win it by his own powers.

. . . All that the ego can do is to create the necessary conditions out of which enlightenment generally arises, but it cannot create this enlightenment itself. By self-purification, by constant aspiration, by regular meditation, by profound study, and by an altruistic attitude in practical life, it does what is prerequisite. But all this is like tapping at the door of the Overself. Only the latter's Grace can open it in the end. . . .

To come into the consciousness of the Overself is an event which can happen only by grace. Yet there is a relation between it and the effort which preceded it. . . .

This moving of consciousness to a higher level will come about by itself, if the calm is patiently allowed to settle itself down sufficiently, and if there has been preparation by study, aspiration, and purification.

Nothing that you do can bring about this wonderful transformation, for it is not the result of effort. It does not depend on the power of your will or the strength of your desire. It is something which can only be done to you, not by you. It is the result of your absorption by another and higher Force. It depends on Grace. It is more elusive yet more satisfying than anything else in life.

. . . The Grace comes in time if it is wanted strongly enough, and then he steps out of the shadows into the sunshine and a benign assurance is born in the heart. Of course this can never be the result of metaphysical striving alone but only of a coordinated, integral effort of thought, feeling, and action. . . .

∽

The period of active effort is at an end; the period of passive waiting now follows it. Without any act on his own part and without any mental movement of his own, the Grace draws him up to the next higher stage and miraculously puts him there where he has so long and so much desired to be. Mark well the absence of self-effort at this stage, how the whole task is taken out of his hands.

∽

Grace works magically on the man who opens himself humbly and sensitively to receive it. His personal feelings undergo a transformation into their higher impersonal octaves. His very weaknesses provoke occasions for gaining effortlessly their opposite virtues. His selfish desires are turned by Grace's alchemy into spiritual aspirations.

∽

A great humility comes into him when at long last he steps aside from his ego sufficiently to allow the perception that it is not in his own power to enter the ultimate Enlightenment. Grace is the arbiter.

∽

When his aspiration rises to an overpowering intensity, it is a sign that Grace is not so far off.

When he has passed successfully through the last trial, overcome the last temptation, and made the last sacrifice of his ego, the reward will be near at hand. The Overself's Grace will become plain, tangible, and wholly embracing.

When all thoughts are extinguished; when even the thought of the quest itself vanishes; when even the final thought of seeking to control thoughts also subsides, then the great battle with the ego can take place. But the last scene of this invisible drama is always played by the Overself. For only when its Grace shoots forth and strikes down this final thought, does success come.

8

Toward a Brighter Future

There is in the very midst of humanity today, albeit hidden and awaiting its hour of manifestation, that which is the very opposite of what has already manifested itself through the evil channels. There is divine pity as against barbarous cruelty, sublime wisdom as against materialistic ignorance, altruistic service as against aggressive selfishness, and exalted reverence against hard atheism. There is the recall to a forgotten God. There is redemptive grace. There is a hand outstretched in mercy to the worst sinner, and in consolation to the worst sufferer. Those who are mystically sensitive feel its presence even now, however intermittently.

These truths, which were formerly kept wholly esoteric and narrowly confined to an intellectually privileged elite, must now be given to the widest possible audience because humanity's position is so precarious. The old secrecy has outlived its usefulness.

∽

. . . the ultimate goal is to discover that there is but one reality, of which all are but a part, that the separateness of the personal ego is but superficial, and that *Truth* is evidenced by the consciousness of unity. The first fruit of such discovery is necessarily the dedication of life to the service of all creatures, to incessant service for universal welfare. . . .

A New World

The message for this age must satisfy its primary needs, hence must contain three elements. First, the *doctrine* that there is a divine soul in man. Second the *gospel* that it is possible through prayer and meditation and study to commune with this soul. Third, the *fact* of the Law of Recompense and hence the necessity of good thoughts and righteous deeds.

∽

The present day needs not only a synthesis of Oriental and Occidental ideas, but also a new creative universal outlook that will transcend both. A world civilization will one day come into being through inward propulsion and outward compulsion. And it will be integral; it will engage all sides of human development. . . .

. . . The time has come to develop the knowledge and extend the understanding of a teaching which few know and fewer still understand. Occupied principally, as it is, with matters of eternal rather than ephemeral life, it finds today a larger opportunity for service than it could have found at any earlier period in consequence of the evolutionary forces which have been working on man's history, ideas, attitudes, communications, and productions. It is the most important knowledge which any human being could study.

. . . If humanity is to travel upward and fulfil its higher destiny, it can do so only by enlarging its area of interest and extending its field of consciousness. It must, in short, seek to realize the Overself on the one hand, to feel its oneness on the other. . . .

The higher purpose of existence is to advance man until he can live in the awareness of his divine selfhood.

This universal message is destined to flow all over the world. Its bearers will be none other than the writings of ancient and modern seers. It will bring people the opportunity to grow, to go forward. . . .

These teachings have first to become known, then understood, next accepted, and lastly made a part of day-to-day living.

Today, the mission of philosophy is a planetary one, for truth is needed everywhere, and for the first time can be transmitted everywhere. . . .

Mankind has entered a new cycle, one wherein each man must learn something of the truth for himself. In former cycles he did not need to bear this responsibility. In the present one, he must accept it.

There is no third way open to us. The world is rapidly moving into a new age. We may either cling to the remnants of the age that is vanishing or we may meet the age which is coming. We must make our choice. . . .

A Truth that Must Be Proclaimed

This is the truth that must be proclaimed to our generation, that the Soul is with us here and now—not in some remote world or distant time, not when the body expires—and that it is our joy and strength to find it.

The immediate task today is for philosophy to deliver its message. The secondary task is to assist those who accept this message to come to a proper and adequate understanding of it. The first is for the multitude and hence public. The second is for the individual and hence private.

The duty to which we are called is not to propagate ideas but to offer them, not to convert reluctant minds but to satisfy hungry ones. . . . There are individuals today to whom these teachings are unknown but who possess in the deeper levels of their mind latent tendencies and beliefs, acquired in former lives, which will leap into forceful activity as soon as the teaching is presented to them.

When the ego discovers that it is a part of the whole, it will naturally cease to live only for its own good and begin to live for the general good also.

. . . Philosophy aims at producing a group of men and women trained in mind control, accustomed to subordinate immediate interests to ultimate ends, sincerely desirous of serving humanity in fundamental ways, and possessed of philosophic knowledge which will make them valuable citizens. . . .

. . . Reverie is not enough. Dream and do. Let the buds of high thought burst into the flowers of heroic action. In the present chaotic and critical state of the world, it is better for those with spiritual ideals to throw their weight into positive service of humanity. We must do something to objectify these ideals.

The needs of this age emphatically demand action in the outer world. Quite a few people of talent, position, vision, or influence have adopted these views, and will take their place in the forefront of things when the destined hour of the New Age sweeps down.

Each person who brings more truth and goodness, more consciousness and balance into his own small circle, brings it into the whole world at the same time. A single individual may be helpless in the face of global events, but the echoes of the echoes of his inspired words and deeds, presence and thoughts, may be heard far from him in place and time.

The best charity in the end is to show a man the higher life that is possible for him.

Whoever by speech or by silence, by art or by example, helps to improve mankind or increase knowledge of the higher truth, renders the best service. No other charity or philanthropy equals this upliftment of creatures struggling—unwittingly or deliberately—to a purified, disciplined, and refined consciousness.

Young persons, whose enthusiasm is fresh and whose minds are open, especially need to become convinced by these teachings. In this way they would not only lay one of the best possible foundations for their future, but also be of the greatest possible service to others.

He who attains even a little power to help others cannot measure where that help will stop. If it gives a lift to one man whom he knows, that man may in his turn give a lift to another person, and so on indefinitely in ever-widening ripples.

. . . The philosophic attitude is that a man shall perform his full duty to the world, but this will be done in such a way that it brings injury to none. Truth, honesty, and honour will not be sacrificed for money. Time, energy, capacity, and money will be used wisely in the best interests of mankind, and above all the philosopher will pray constantly that the Overself will accept him as a dedicated instrument of service. And it surely will.

Those who are searching for truth are only a small number but still they are a growing number. Each of us may repay his own obligation by saying *the right word at the right time,* by lending or giving the right book to the truth-hungry person.

. . . you are to enter a new and different rhythm and tell such as will listen that they need not be forlorn, lost, or without hope because they find none to appeal to their heart or mind. They are asked only to follow *the God within themselves,* for "The Kingdom of Heaven is within you." . . .

As the consciousness of the Overself seeps into him, the power of the Overself expresses through him.

Whoever has benefited by these ideas is under an obligation to make them available to whoever else may be ready to receive them. . . .

Whoever keeps this divine flame burning brightly within his heart, radiates the spirit of his purpose to all whom he contacts.

A true power will inform the hands of those who will act at the behest of the god within, whose daily admonishment to him is: "Go out and live for the welfare of man the Light you find in the deep recesses of your own heart."

The wonder and joy of finding himself to be a channel of blessing, teaching, healing peace, and uplift to others will increase as the results themselves increase.

❦

...I am *never really alone* when writing but every now and then there rises before my mind's eye the vision of some man or woman whose whole life may take a new and nobler course because of a few paragraphs which flow lightly from this old pen of mine. . . .

The Works of Paul Brunton

(See http://paulbrunton.org for descriptions.)

Early Publications

A Search in Secret India
The Secret Path
A Search in Secret Egypt
A Message from Arunachala
A Hermit in the Himalayas
The Quest of the Overself
The Inner Reality (Discover Yourself)
Indian Philosophy and Modern Culture
The Hidden Teaching beyond Yoga
The Wisdom of the Overself
The Spiritual Crisis of Man

Published posthumously

Essays on the Quest

The Notebooks of Paul Brunton, in 16 volumes

1: Perspectives
2: The Quest
3: Practices for the Quest; Relax and Retreat
4: Meditation; The Body
5: Emotions and Ethics; The Intellect
6: The Ego; From Birth to Rebirth
7: Healing of the Self; The Negatives
8: Reflections on My Life and Writings
9: Human Experience; The Arts in Culture
10: The Orient
11: The Sensitives
12: The Religious Urge; The Reverential Life
13: Relativity, Philosophy, and Mind
14: Inspiration and the Overself
15: Advanced Contemplation; The Peace Within You
16: Enlightened Mind, Divine Mind

Also